Praise for *Brain Changer*

"A superb practical primer for thinking about thinking."

—ROBERT A. BURTON, MD,
author of *On Being Certain* and *A Skeptic's Guide to the Mind*

❋

"Forget the self-help mumbo jumbo, DiSalvo boils down decades of actual research from psychological laboratories while giving us proven, scientist-approved tips on how to easily harness our maximum brainpower. From chewing gum, to writing our own obituaries, to gargling with lemonade, you'll be amazed by the many ways you can rev up that powerful engine puttering along in your cranium."

—JESSE BERING, PHD,
author of *The Belief Instinct* and contributor to *Scientific American* and *Slate*

"David DiSalvo will change the way you think about your own thinking, and in the process provide you with practical tools for keeping life's challenges in perspective."

—WRAY HERBERT,
author of *On Second Thought: Outsmarting Your Mind's Hard-Wired Habits*

❋

"DiSalvo beautifully breaks down metacognition—our ability to reflect back upon our own thought processes—and, just as capably, lays out all the ways in which it can be sharpened for greater psychological well-being. An engaging and scientifically grounded read."

—ALICE G. WALTON, PHD,
contributing writer to the American Psychological Association and *Forbes*

❋

"An awareness of the under-the-surface workings of your own brain helps you adapt wisely to challenging circumstances, and *Brain Changer* offers just such an awareness. DiSalvo shows you how to exert more conscious control over your own thinking processes for better problem solving and decision making."

—SUSAN K. PERRY, PhD,
author of *Writing in Flow* and contributor to *Psychology Today*

✳

"I believe the greatest competitive advantage any professional can gain today is a better understanding of how to leverage brainpower. Not only has David DiSalvo opened up pathways that I never knew existed; more importantly, he gave me the power to see my world from a far greater, more inspiring perspective."

—MOE ABDOU,
founder of 33voices.com, a global conversation about things that matter in business and in life

Praise for David DiSalvo and *What Makes Your Brain Happy and Why You Should Do the Opposite* and *The Brain in Your Kitchen*

"David DiSalvo takes us on a whistle-stop tour of our mind's delusions. No aspect of daily life is left untouched: whether he is exploring job interviews, first dates, or the perils of eBay, DiSalvo will change the way you think about thinking…an enjoyable manual to your psyche that may change your life."

—*NEW SCIENTIST*

✳

"DiSalvo offers 'science-help' (as opposed to self-help) by detailing the mental shortcuts our minds like to take but that don't always serve us well, with the assumption that understanding brain function helps us fight its stubborn behavior."

—*PSYCHOLOGY TODAY*

✳

"The expression 'knowledge is power' has never been more appropriate. Mr. DiSalvo takes the mystery out of our daily self-sabotage. Using science and psychology he leads us into awareness and provides us action steps to make our lives better."

—*New York Journal of Books*

✱

"Lots of books tell you what you should do to be happy. But call me thorough—I like to know what not to do, too. Science writer David DiSalvo fills out the 'happiness' category with insights into why we pursue things that don't really make us happy…you will learn a lot about the self-destructive behaviors that keep you from being fulfilled."

—*The Huffington Post*

✱

"By weaving together the latest studies, science writer DiSalvo examines why people's desires often thwart their goals."

—*Science News*

✱

"A really fascinating look into the workings of the brain, combining a physiological and psychological model, with chapters that are linked together like literary sausages, making it hard to put the book down."

—*San Francisco Book Review*

✱

"A comprehensive overview of the latest in psychology and neuroscience developments, backed by experiments conducted on each point…well-written and highly recommended."

—*Portland Book Review*

✱

"David DiSalvo is our go-to source for true facts about the human brain. Whatever the brain is up to, and often it's up to something tricky, you can rest assured that DiSalvo will be keeping an eye on it, and a skeptical eye at that."

—JEFF MCMAHON,
University of Chicago lecturer, editor of *Contrary* magazine, and contributor to *Forbes*

✻

"Every week the media delivers to the public a barrage of psychology and neuroscience findings. They sound fascinating, but are untethered from daily life. David DiSalvo extracts the practical potential of these discoveries, and in so doing performs a public service that is creative and witty."

— J. D. TROUT, PhD,
author of *The Empathy Gap: Building Bridges to the Good Life and the Good Society*, and Professor of Philosophy and Psychology, Loyola University Chicago

✻

"David DiSalvo provides an unusually well-written foray into the fascinating fields of neuroscience and social psychology. He will pique your curiosity and help you understand people in new ways."

— CHARLES H. ELLIOTT, PhD,
coauthor of nine psychology books, including *Overcoming Anxiety for Dummies, Obsessive-Compulsive Disorder for Dummies,* and *Borderline Personality Disorder for Dummies*

✻

"DiSalvo takes us on a refreshing voyage into the multitude of ways your brain is busy smacking you around, and provides an antidote to the standard servings of self-help snake oil."

— MARK CHANGIZI, PhD,
author of *Harnessed: How Language and Music Mimicked Nature and Transformed Ape to Man*

✻

"DiSalvo delivers a levelheaded, healthy skepticism as he brings the light of evidence to bear. He has a knack for knowing 'how much is too much' in the way of scientific jargon and has created very readable yet informative books that leave the reader feeling confident and informed."

—ROBERT VANDERVOORT, PharmD,
Pharmacotherapy Faculty, Florida Hospital

✻

"DiSalvo uses the raw ingredients of science and research to cook practical advice. He presents us with what we know, and just as important, what we do not know about how our brains, which evolved to survive scarcity and lack, can survive in a world awash with excess of every type."

— TODD ESSIG, PhD,
clinical psychologist and author of the Managing Mental Wealth column at *Forbes*

✻

"Reading DiSalvo is like eating intellectual dim sum at your favorite Chinese restaurant. Each morsel is tasty and you will keep coming back for more."

— BRUCE M. HOOD, PhD,
author of *SuperSense: Why We Believe in the Unbelievable* and *The Self Illusion: How the Social Brain Creates Identity,* and Director of the University of Bristol Cognitive Development Center

✻

"[DiSalvo's] book is packed full of scientific insights with practical applications to everyday life—a thought-provoking and entertaining page-turner."

— **GARY SMALL, MD,**
UCLA Professor of Psychiatry, author of *The Memory Bible* and coauthor of *iBrain: Surviving the Technological Alteration of the Modern Mind* and *The Naked Lady Who Stood on Her Head: A Psychiatrist's Stories of His Most Bizarre Cases*

✳

"DiSalvo's book will make your brain happy—in a good way. With engaging prose and compelling stories, DiSalvo provides a fast-paced overview of mental shortcuts and foibles that make us happy in the short-term, often to our long-term detriment."

— **DANIEL SIMONS, PhD,**
Professor of Psychology at the University of Illinois and coauthor of *The Invisible Gorilla: And Other Ways Our Intuitions Deceive Us*

✳

"The Swiss Army knife of psychology and neuroscience research—handy, practical, and very, very useful. [DiSalvo] boils down the latest findings into simple easy-to-understand lessons you can apply to your daily life."

—**JOSEPH T. HALLINAN,**
Pulitzer Prize-winning journalist and author of *Why We Make Mistakes*

✳

"A well-researched and effectively argued guide to uncovering the reasons why we so often think and act in ways that undermine our best interests...full of knowledge about why humans manipulate each other. If you want to know more about why you do what you do, and how to avoid becoming the victim of someone else's manipulation tactics, I encourage you to read this book."

— **PHILIP ZIMBARDO, PhD,**
author of *The Lucifer Effect: Understanding How Good People Turn Evil*, and past president of the American Psychological Association

✻

"David DiSalvo's gleanings from current neuroscience and psychology are entertaining, intriguing, and instructive."

— **JOSEPH CARROLL, PhD,**
author of *Reading Human Nature: Literary Darwinism in Theory and Practice*

✻

"Science writer DiSalvo points out that many of our actions that make our brains 'happy' actually place roadblocks in our way. With input from many of the top thinkers in psychology and neuroscience, he offers helpful strategies to avoid pitfalls."

—*THE SACRAMENTO BEE*

✻

"With one eye on neuroscience and the other on cognitive psychology, David DiSalvo reveals what's 'behind the curtain' when it comes to common self-defeating human behaviors…written in an engaging yet erudite style anyone can grasp."

—*GOOD READS*

✻

"Selectively—but incisively—reviewing recent cognitive science research, this eminently useful work illustrates the many ways that the human brain's surprising neuroplasticity can be productively exploited. Cogently optimistic about our potential to alter negative thoughts and actions, DiSalvo delineates simple but powerful ways to effect such beneficial cognitive/behavioral change."

—LEON F. SELTZER, PhD,
author of *Paradoxical Strategies in Psychotherapy: A Comprehensive Overview and Guidebook*

BRAIN CHANGER

AUTHOR OF
What Makes Your Brain Happy and Why You Should Do the Opposite
and *The Brain in Your Kitchen*

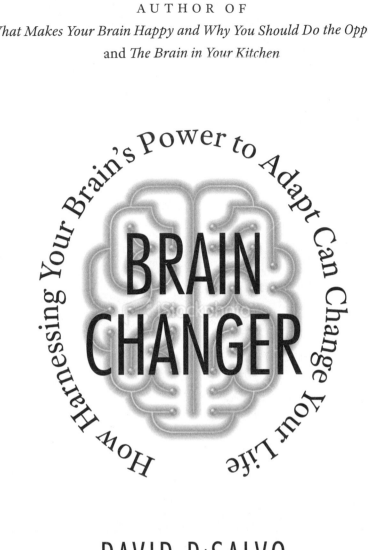

How Harnessing Your Brain's Power to Adapt Can Change Your Life

BRAIN CHANGER

DAVID DiSALVO

BENBELLA BOOKS

DALLAS, TEXAS

BenBella Books, Inc.
10300 N. Central Expressway, Suite 530
Dallas, TX 75231
www.benbellabooks.com
Send feedback to feedback@benbellabooks.com

Printed in the United States of America
10 9 8 7 6 5 4 3 2 1

Library of Congress Cataloging-in-Publication Data
DiSalvo, David, 1970-
    Brain changer : how harnessing your brain's power to adapt can change your life / David DiSalvo.
        pages cm
    Includes bibliographical references and index.
    ISBN 978-1-939529-00-8 (pbk.) — ISBN 978-1-939529-01-5
1. Metacognition. 2. Self-actualization (Psychology) 3. Neurosciences. I. Title.
    BF311.D5373 2013
    153—dc23
    2013026317

Editing by Eric Wechter
Copyediting by Annie Gottlieb
Proofreading by Kimberly Marini and
    Kristin Vorce
Cover design by Sarah Dombrowsky
Artwork and conceptual integration by
    Donald Wilson Bush, Illustrator

Text design by John Reinhardt Book
    Design
Text composition by Integra Software
    Services Pvt. Ltd
Printed by Bang Printing

Distributed by Perseus Distribution
To place orders through Perseus Distribution:
Tel: (800) 343-4499
Fax: (800) 351-5073
E-mail: orderentry@perseusbooks.com
www.perseusdistribution.com

Significant discounts for bulk sales are available. Please contact Glenn Yeffeth at glenn@benbellabooks.com or (214) 750-3628.

In memory of my dad,
Louis DiSalvo

.

CONTENTS

PART III: EXPAND

APPENDICES

FOREWORD

WHAT WE CALL OUR DESTINY IS TRULY OUR CHARACTER AND THAT
CHARACTER CAN BE ALTERED . . . IF WE HAVE THE COURAGE TO EXAMINE
HOW IT FORMED US. WE CAN ALTER THE CHEMISTRY PROVIDED WE
HAVE THE COURAGE TO DISSECT THE ELEMENTS.

— *Anaïs Nin*

O F REINCARNATION, the ancient Hindus once said that true nobil-
ity comes not from being superior to others, but, rather, from
being superior to our previous selves. The modern response is,
why wait for the next round? In this life—right *now,* actually—we want
better. Our relationships are souring; we're eating too many sweets;
we're stuck in dead-end jobs. We seek the open road; we want to master the art of small talk; we want our discourse to be meaningful; we
believe in purpose and in the pursuit of happiness, too. More highs,
fewer lows, less stress—that's the goal.

The problem? We have no idea how to achieve these noble goals—
and most self-help philosophies offer succor, not success . . . at least
not the type that sticks. (How else can an $11 billion industry keep

sustaining itself?) Our goals may be well defined, but the path certainly isn't. Five pounds forward, five pounds back. One rung higher on the career ladder, two happiness steps back. Worse, the very part of ourselves that seeks to fix our problems is elusive: it's assertive one moment, absent the next. How can we save this tiny bootstrap-believing sliver of ourselves from the self-sabotaging majority?

A case in point: I'm writing in the café of a trendy yoga center in New York City. At the table next to me are two women. Both are beautiful: taut, glowing; even their hair is radiant. You can see that they've put themselves on the path to enlightenment. But their postures and facial expressions betray them. One yogini has been talking about her boyfriend (he's traveling too much and she caught him lying). Her friend is getting angry and indignant. Back and forth the two go, rehashing bad-boyfriend scenarios over and over again to a point of exhaustion. They've effectively canceled out their entire yoga session. (Studies confirm: when girlfriends talk with one another excessively about problems, their cortisol levels skyrocket. Physiologically, they're experiencing the stressor over and over again.)

So, how do we stop the self-subversion?

The answer lies in understanding how the brain works. Improving ourselves *by thinking about our thinking* is the possibility at the center of David DiSalvo's *Brain Changer*. To go about this, as detailed in the pages that follow, is to see our brains as a confluence of *feedback loops*.

The idea of feedback goes back to the Industrial Revolution, when it was coined to describe the regulatory mechanisms of complex machinery (if your steam engine is overheating it must cycle down to maintain its cool). But the expression first came into popular use in the 1940s, when the mathematician Norbert Wiener applied it to all adaptive systems: biological, mechanical, political, and social. In his pioneering book *The Human Use of Human Beings*, he wrote:

> Feedback [is] the property of being able to adjust future conduct
> by past performance. Feedback may be as simple as that of the
> common reflex, or it may be a higher order feedback, in which

past experience is used not only to regulate specific movements, but also whole policies of behavior.

Feedback is like karma: what goes around, comes around. It includes our interactions with others; our internal dialogues; and the exchange between conscious and unconscious thoughts. These exchanges have a chemical basis—serotonin, dopamine, glutamate, which are themselves subject to feedback loops. Loops upon loops upon loops.

By itself, feedback doesn't drive self-improvement. (We've all been trapped in destructive thought patterns. And introspection by itself doesn't work, especially when it drives us into a rumination rut, as we now know from recent studies.)

The goal here is the purpose-driven loop: *thinking about thinking* with the intent to gain more control over those thoughts. How? By detaching ourselves from problems, learning, self-correcting, and, ultimately, *adapting*. Since the key is more conscious control over our thought processes, there's good news: our tools are improving. Behavioral studies, brain scans, hormone tests—they've all helped researchers identify techniques that can change our minds in the desired ways. Drawing on research in behavioral psychology and cognitive science, *Brain Changer* introduces strategies for tweaking the brain's motivation-and-reward centers and overcoming cognitive biases. In effect, we learn to identify our sweet spots and see our blind spots. (This book and DiSalvo's previous title, *What Makes Your Brain Happy and Why You Should Do the Opposite*, fall into a promising new category coined by the author: science-help.)

The second section of this book offers a buffet of brain-changer techniques, and they're all compelling: how to drown out inner noise, cultivate inner silence, sync with other brains, and increase our metaphor quotient, among many others. (They all require work—some more than others. No one said that brain changing is easy.)

For me, the most useful, all-purpose brain changer is the "awareness wedge." It involves a moment of self-reflection in the heat of a moment—just enough time to leverage some influence over the xx ❄ BRAIN CHANGER

outcome. In that beat or two we redirect our thoughts in specific ways that DiSalvo describes—including short-circuiting anger responses and questioning existing patterns. You can imagine how helpful this strategy would be in times of stress, anxiety, and outrage. The women at the yoga center would've kept their radiant cool had they discussed the problem, then stopped themselves and refocused their energy on finding a solution. That pause—it's a moment of grace.

Science still hasn't pinpointed what the self is—if that elusive entity (or entities?) can ever truly be isolated. ("There are three things extremely hard: steel, a diamond, and to know one's self," Benjamin Franklin said.) But DiSalvo writes about what the self can do: process 40 pieces of information a second consciously (11 million per second unconsciously). This is astounding processing power. Imagine what that sliver of self-awareness could do if it becomes better at thinking about its thinking: when it can pull itself out of negative cycles and launch decisive new ones, adapt, and become more flexible and resilient all the while.

Loops upon loops upon loops.

— Jena Pincott, science writer, author of *Do Gentleman Really Prefer Blondes* and *Do Chocolate Lovers Have Sweeter Babies?: The Surprising Science of Pregnancy*

PREFACE

RETHINK

Do not weep; do not wax indignant. Understand.

—*Baruch Spinoza*

MARK HAD BEEN feeling a little dizzy for most of the morning, but assumed he might just be fighting off a virus. He was an athletic, undeniably healthy guy not prone to getting sick, and some minor dizziness didn't concern him. That is, until this particular bout of dizziness morphed into something altogether different. By early afternoon Mark found it hard to stand up without feeling like he'd immediately drop to the floor. Just before 3:00 p.m., he lost feeling in his right leg, soon followed by numbness throughout his right arm—and then an inability to move almost at all.

His wife, Jessica, rushed him to the hospital and quickly called his brother, who left work early and got there before them. He didn't understand it—just yesterday, he and Mark had been grilling hamburgers and kicking a soccer ball around (a sport Mark not only played but coached as well), and Mark was his usual energetic self. What could have happened in less than twenty-four hours? When he saw his brother, his bewilderment shifted to terror. Mark was frozen, barely able to move his mouth to say a single word, and the entire right side of his body was motionless as if cast in invisible concrete.

The attending doctor asked if Mark had been working with toxic fumes, had accidentally ingested anything poisonous, or had possibly been bitten by a snake or spider. The answer was "no" across the board. Mark had slept in a little that morning—not unusual for a Saturday— and after that the extent of his activity had been reading the newspaper and playing with the dog. He had not been sick for months before this, aside from a sinus infection he'd developed after surfing all day, which was quickly quelled by antibiotics.

A neurologist was brought in to evaluate, and his preliminary diagnosis was not good. Mark was most likely suffering from a brain tumor, the neurologist told Jessica and Mark's brother. He needed to be rushed to a hospital better equipped to handle it. Within a half hour Mark was in an ambulance racing to another hospital. The neurologist told Jessica that the medley of drastic symptoms Mark was experiencing indicated that his chances of recovery might be very slim, and she should be prepared for the worst.

At the new hospital, two more neurologists evaluated Mark. One concurred with the diagnosis of a tumor, but the other wasn't so sure. An MRI clearly showed an abnormality in the left hemisphere of Mark's brain, but precisely what the abnormality was wasn't clear at all. It could be a tumor, but it might also be damage caused by an aneurysm, or possibly a different sort of lesion altogether. They did agree, however, that Mark would have to undergo emergency brain surgery. With his paralysis worsening, and with very little to go by except for a questionable MRI scan, surgery was the best option to determine exactly what had struck down a healthy thirty-three-year-old man without warning.

Five hours of surgery revealed a cause that no one had considered: Mark's brain was in the throes of an aggressive bacterial infection. It had spread so rapidly that multiple areas of his brain were already affected, causing a series of damaging micro-strokes. Left untreated, he would likely have died within hours. Mark was put on a cocktail of powerful antibiotics, fed into his system continuously by a series of intravenous pumps.

Two days after surgery the infection had not abated. But in the coming days it gradually weakened. After a full week of lying incapacitated in a hospital bed with tubes spanning from one side of the room to the other, Mark's body was finally gaining the upper hand over the infection. By day nine, he was able to sit up in bed with assistance, though the paralysis on his right side remained.

Fortunately, he was once again able to speak, and his words reassured Jessica and many visitors that he was indeed feeling much better. In a few days, he was able to stand—again with assistance— and balance himself upright by shifting his weight to his left side. Though the situation remained far from ideal, standing at all was quite an accomplishment, and Mark was visibly pleased that he could manage it.

One morning in the hospital room, Mark pushed himself up from the bed with his left arm and actually stood without assistance. Jessica almost couldn't believe it, but she knew her husband's determination, and knew he would start forging ahead to recovery as soon as he was the least bit able.

Then, just as he seemed to be starting on that upward-bound road, something happened. Mark fell back onto the bed, but not because he'd lost his balance. He fell as if he'd been shot—all at once, a complete collapse. He was unconscious and Jessica tried to wake him, thinking perhaps the strain of standing had been too much in his weakened condition. Nurses ran into the room, checked his vital signs, and Mark was rushed to intensive care on a gurney. Within minutes he was being prepped for emergency surgery. Mark had suffered a major heart attack.

Again Jessica was told to prepare for the worst. The cause of Mark's attack, the doctors said, wasn't entirely clear. But no matter how the attack was related to his original condition, Mark was once again fighting for his life.

The heart surgery lasted six hours, and concluded with the best possible outcome—Mark pulled through. He would now have several days ahead of recovering from the surgery, even as he was still not fully recovered from the brain infection. The path that had appeared to be getting a little easier once again became harder than anything Mark could have imagined just two weeks before.

When Mark was finally released from the hospital weeks later, he struggled to fathom how his life had changed in an instant. On a typical Saturday morning he'd felt a little dizzy. Now he was partially paralyzed, a survivor of brain surgery and open-heart surgery.

Even beyond the physical outcomes, he faced a formidable group of mental obstacles catalyzed by the abrupt shattering of life as he knew it. More than once he asked himself, "How can I deal with this?" His doctors told him that under the best conditions, after months of physical therapy, he would regain only 50 percent use of his right arm and leg. That meant that a major part of Mark's life—sports and physical activity—was going to radically change. To do anything approaching what he'd been able to do before the infection set in, he was facing a mountain range of recovery. But no matter how hard he worked, he knew that he'd have to come to terms with the reality of simply not being the person he used to be. His emotions bounded to extremes: sadness to hopelessness; disappointment to anger.

Added to it all was a question that no doctor—not even nationally regarded epidemiologists brought in to study the case—could answer: How did the infection strike so far and deeply into his brain? Mark's case was a true anomaly. The type of infection that had nearly killed him was not supposed to be able to pass through the blood-brain barrier—and yet, despite stacks of medical research to the contrary, it had.

The open-endedness of the question underlined Mark's growing realization that certainty and stability were figments—if this could happen, then anything could happen. All things considered, Mark's mental outlook was damaged at least as much as his physical outlook.

Mark went through many dark times in the months after he was released from the hospital, returning to a world that seemed almost foreign now. He suffered bouts of depression, and for periods—sometimes days at a time—he didn't want to leave his house, or even his sofa. But Mark didn't drop anchor and stay in the dark. He took one immensely significant step that was the difference between sinking deeper, or emerging to work through the obstacles. He challenged himself at the very core of everything—his thinking. Mark stepped outside himself and gained perspective on the destructive thought process that was taking over, and then—like a journalist covering a story about his mind—he began deconstructing those thoughts. He challenged every part of the thought process—the dire assumptions he was making, the delusions of inevitability he'd succumbed to, and the pernicious thought that if he couldn't be who he was before, then he simply couldn't be.

Mark also learned that the harder he tried to repress his feelings about what he was facing, the more they erupted and pulled energy away from the constructive work he'd started. So he stopped trying to control them and allowed himself to experience and identify those feelings; as he did, each lost a little more of its intensity.

There is nothing clear-cut about the challenge Mark was facing. Self-examination is messy at best, and fraught with more setbacks than advances. But what's crucial is that Mark didn't give up on the challenge to change his thinking. No matter how long it would take, he wasn't about to back off. And he never did.

The true conclusion to this true story is that Mark struggled through success and failure to think differently about his new situation and the changes he'd have to embrace to adapt to a different kind of life. Doing so opened the mental door to the hard work ahead. He pushed himself through physical recovery to gain as much use of his arm and leg as possible, even though the outcome was just as the doctors told him it would be: roughly half the control he'd had before. Mark and Jessica went on to start a family as they'd planned, and he became the father of a beautiful little girl. He eventually returned to coaching soccer at the school where he taught, and within a year he was even able to get on a surfboard again.[1]

Most of us will never have to overcome the obstacles that Mark faced. Most of our lives won't be interrupted so abruptly, and most of us won't have to know what it feels like to adapt to a drastically different life than we knew only weeks before.

Mark's situation is atypical, but it offers an example that all of us can learn from—a blueprint for what is necessary to overcome the obstacles that immediately appear whenever we are trying to push ahead, achieve, and accomplish. Sometimes those obstacles are small; other times they appear insurmountable. But the overriding truth is that we all face them, and how we "think about our thinking"—a practice known as *metacognition*—will make the difference between an outcome that leaves us wanting and one that is fulfilling.

And that's where this book begins. In every part of our lives we face this challenge of self-reflection—and we are fortunate to live in an age when the disciplines within psychology and cognitive science are beginning to offer evidence-based knowledge clues for taking on the challenge. Science-help, rather than typical self-help, provides a grounded approach to asking hard questions about ourselves, and evaluating our thinking at a deeper level than previously possible.

The results will not always be to our liking; thinking, after all, is a chaotic business. But like Mark, we are wise to forge ahead and tenaciously manage the chaos if what we want to accomplish is truly important to us.

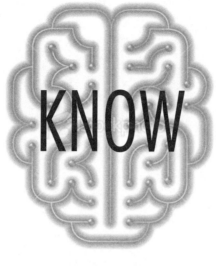

KNOW

DO

EXPAND

INTRODUCTION

BRAIN CHANGING

THE MIND SHIFT HAS BEGUN

THINGS DO NOT CHANGE; WE CHANGE.

—*Henry David Thoreau*

You AND I are about to embark upon something philosophers are fond of calling a "thought experiment." Don't get me wrong—this won't be a philosophical exercise in the academic sense. Testing the bounds of rhetoric and wandering the labyrinths of logical fallacies won't help us reach our goal. This experiment is, in the best sense of the term, pragmatic.

Taking on the roles of curious adventurers—thirsty, perhaps unquenchably so, to know more—we are going to use the tools science has given us and go to work. Our experiment won't take place in a research lab, though we'll consult numerous researchers along the way. Together we are going to figure out how *it* works, why *it* works, and, most importantly, the implications of changing how *it* works.

How what works? The "it" of our pragmatic endeavor is nothing less than the glorious marvel of nature that sits just behind our eyes, the reaches of which extend throughout our nervous system. Indeed, when discussing our brain, it's no exaggeration to say that we're talking about our body overall, because no part of us operates outside its influence. And when we speak of our mind, as we shall see, the definition expands yet further.

The Mind Shift

A few decades ago, two schools of scientific thought about the human mind began integrating, and this synthesis of disciplines has created a profound new understanding that continues to transform our culture today.

The first school, cognitive science, brought to the table an emphasis on understanding how the human brain yields consciousness and how thinking drives emotions. The second school, behavioral science, emphasizes what human behavior reveals about how the mind works and how social enculturation influences thinking.

Both of these schools, at least in their modern forms, are relatively new on the scientific scene, so it isn't surprising that they developed on parallel paths for a few seasons before those paths intersected. When they did, a wealth of combined knowledge and technologies reshaped our understanding of consciousness, thinking, emotion, social behavior, and virtually everything else related to the brain and nervous system. Enhancing our understanding even further, disciplines such as evolutionary psychology, social neuroscience, and behavioral economics have recently joined the party as well.

What has changed since this integration began is impossible to capture in any one book, or even a shelf of books, but here are a few of the highlights:

- The brain is no longer considered a static organ that stops changing after childhood. We now know that it changes throughout our lives; that it is, in a sense, "plastic"—hence the now well-accepted term "neuroplasticity."

- Brain functions such as memory and learning don't emerge and operate from one specific brain area; they are distributed across multiple brain areas that connect through a ceaseless symphony of neurochemical exchanges.

- The roles of the left and right hemispheres of the brain are not nearly as distinct and unrelated as previously thought, but are instead complementary actors on the same stage whose roles converge in endless feedback loops.

- Personality, once thought unchangeable, turns out to be remarkably malleable, and strict personality categories like "introvert" and "extrovert" are not the impermeable silos we used to think they were (in fact, most of us fall in between—defining the majority of humans more accurately as ambiverts).

- Humans are not "rational actors." In fact, we're seldom aware of the influences, biases, and distortions that affect how we think and act.

- The unconscious is not Freud's cauldron of seething unmet needs, wants, and desires, but instead an almost incomprehensibly complex composite of processing "modules" that control almost everything we do day in and day out; consciousness, by comparison, is a miniscule domain.

- Our minds are what our brains do, but they're also what other brains do; humans are mind-synced in ways we never realized.

These brief examples give you a just a taste of what has changed in a short time. We've made more progress in understanding the brain and mind in the last thirty years than in all of the time leading up to that point.

This book addresses the question "How does 'the Mind Shift,' as I call it, affect all of us?"

Where Do You Live Along the Fault Line?

Most of us don't read research papers in academic journals to learn about the latest neuroscientific findings. Our daily routines seemingly insulate us from concerns about what scientific school is doing what with whom and where. If it really mattered, someone would tell us about it, right?

Well, it matters, and the book you're reading will explain why. What it comes down to is whether you will benefit from the Mind Shift or not: whether your life will be enriched by the new science-based findings about the brain, or whether you'll remain indifferent. The path of least resistance is apathy. I hope to convince you that the "apathy of mind" camp is not a good place to set up your tepee. If you do, you can expect to be on the receiving end of the other side's influence with ever-increasing frequency. The reason why is deceptively simple: *they will be better thinkers than you.*

But Before We Really Start Wrestling with the Details...

Let's set the tone for our journey together. First things first: Who am I and why did I write this book?

First, what I am not: I'm not a psychiatrist, psychologist, neuroscientist, academic researcher, or study-hall lecturer. I am a science writer with an insatiable curiosity about how our brains work and a compulsion to communicate what I learn to anyone as curious as I am.

I write about science and technology topics for magazines large and small, including *Scientific American Mind*, *Forbes*, *Psychology Today*, and *Mental Floss*, and for newspapers such as *The Wall Street Journal*. I write a regular blog called *The Daily Brain*, and I've written a book called *What Makes Your Brain Happy and Why You Should Do the Opposite*.

In that book (written on the foundation of "science-help"—more on that later), I focused on a topic most often referred to as "cognitive bias." I wanted to explore the reasons we so often think and act in ways that don't serve our best interests, and what it is about our brains—incredible organs though they are—that makes getting out of our own way so difficult. The book elaborates on the many biases, distortions, and delusions each of us trips over to varying degrees, and offers suggestions, drawn from cognitive-science research, on how to overcome these obstacles.

This book doesn't re-cover that territory, and not just because it's already been covered. We have a bigger, broader, and—dare I say—more enjoyable endeavor before us.

Since writing my first book and countless subsequent articles about the brain, I have become an inveterate optimist about the possibility of change. To put that statement in context, I should tell you that I consider myself a rational skeptic about most topics, and I'm not easily convinced.

When you write in the science and technology fields long enough, you learn to distinguish the veneer of truth from the genuine article. Sadly, there's far more veneer than the good stuff out there. There are also more people trying to convince you that what they are promoting is worth your time (and money) than there are people sincerely doing the hard work of, well, just trying to figure things out.

But when it comes to the subjects in this book, I am an optimist—and I consider my optimism to be tried, tested, and intact. I feel quite strongly that as you continue reading, you'll adopt a similar mindset, and my hope is that by the end of this book you'll be as energized and hopeful as I am.

What is the source of my optimism?

Here's the headline version: we now understand the underlying principles of how our brains work and interact with our environments.

In terms of thought and action, the cognitive and behavioral sciences have provided us with innovative ways to think about the brain. In the last few decades, and particularly the last few years, we have uncovered incredible things about our brains—and by extension, our minds.

At the core is an understanding that our brains house constellations of never-ending "feedback loops," operating together as a conceptual engine that drives our thoughts and behaviors. By better understanding feedback loops and the dynamics that affect them, we are positioned to understand how to change thought and behavior—an inspiring prospect by any measure.

So that gives you a flavor of my optimism, a glimpse into a story that has been captivating my attention and driving my passion for years. But lest you think you've happened upon a "nuts and bolts" book about the brain—a sort of watchmaker's guide to gear ratios and timing adjustments—let me add a few more clarifications.

All of the discussions in this book have neurochemical underpinnings. In other words, nothing in our brains occurs independently of the endless exchanges of crucial chemicals such as dopamine, serotonin, and glutamate, to name just a few. To really understand how the brain works, it's important to understand those chemicals and their roles. We can say almost nothing about why we are driven to achieve goals, for example, without referring to the indispensable role of dopamine in our brain's aptly labeled "reward center".[1]

Having said that, the endeavor we're embarking on together is not an exercise in brain anatomy and neurochemical intrigue. We're going to pay deference to the chemical drama of our greatest organ without making it our feature presentation. Where it is important to understand how particular chemicals interact, due diligence will be served. But this isn't a neuroscience textbook. Remember, this book has a pragmatic objective: to present the possibility of change.

Many books in the traditional self-help genre attempt to provide a system or formula for success. They describe a problem, offer the solution, and tell you how to get from A to B. My experience as a science writer—and a public education specialist before that—inoculates me against buying into success formulas. I just don't see the world that way, and that's why I say that I write "science-help" instead of self-help. Science-help draws knowledge clues from research to understand problems and propose solutions.[2]

I am not an "I found the answer!" sort of person, and this isn't that sort of book. As I said up front, we're undertaking a thought experiment together. We're building our awareness, exploring ways to turn that awareness into action.

In doing so, we are searching for the possibility of change—change that I am extremely optimistic about. But we always have to remember that science isn't about answers. It's about questions. If we're going to use the tools of science to do the work of exploring, then we have to acknowledge the rules of science as well, the most important of which is that we do not fool ourselves into thinking we've "nailed it" once and for all.

Does that mean we can't discover truths, and, practically speaking, make use of them in our lives? Of course not; books like this one would never be written if that were the case. It simply means that we have to be careful about adopting a courtroom mentality—concluding that we've settled the case and can move on. Instead, I think we should hope to settle a few parts of the "case," and also open brand-new ones—which will captivate us, moving forward, as much as or more than their forerunners.

With those tone-setters and clarifications behind us, let's talk a bit about what's coming next—the good stuff.

I've briefly mentioned feedback loops, and as we continue forward they will serve as the central metaphor guiding our journey. To put a finer point on that:

FEEDBACK LOOPS ARE THE ENGINES OF YOUR ADAPTIVE BRAIN.

We're also going to discuss what I consider to be the driving dynamic of the conscious mind. Cognitive scientists call it metacognition. In the simplest definition, and the one that will serve us best, metacognition means "thinking about thinking." Why is that so important? Because...

METACOGNITION IS THE MOST POWERFUL INTERNAL FORCE WE POSSESS TO INFLUENCE FEEDBACK LOOPS.

With those broad strokes as background, the book is broken out into three main parts, with several subsections.

Part I—Know: Here we'll walk through the working dynamics of the mindscape—in both conscious mind space and the vast processing universe called the unconscious.

Part II—Do: Here we'll move from knowledge to action. *Do* includes a selection of thinking tools to enhance our thinking abilities and catalyze action.

Part III—Expand: In this final section we'll review a wide variety of excellent sources: nonfiction, fiction, and movies—a selection chosen to expand upon what we've explored throughout the book.

Let's begin our exploration—this pragmatic thought experiment rooted in well-considered optimism. The only requirements on your part are openness to possibilities and willingness to be inspired.

METACOGNITION

THE IMPASSIVE WATCHER
IN THE TOWER

THE ULTIMATE VALUE OF LIFE DEPENDS UPON AWARENESS AND THE
POWER OF CONTEMPLATION RATHER THAN UPON MERE SURVIVAL.

—*Aristotle*

W E BEGIN OUR DISCUSSION with a graphic, one that we'll revisit
throughout the book as a sort of visual anchor for the concepts
central to metacognition, adaptation, and major looping highways in between. The first stop is at the top: *defining metacognition
itself.*

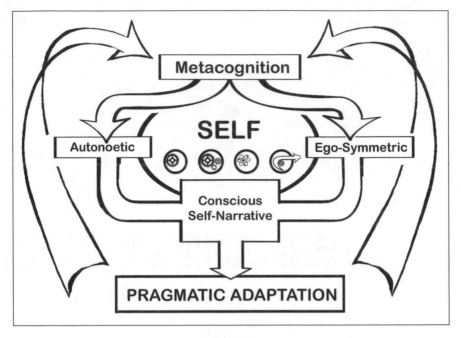

FIGURE 1.1

What Is Metacognition?

Problem-solving techniques —like those used in a variety of cognitive and behavioral therapies, for example—rely on a tool unique to humans, one that we use all the time (albeit intuitively, without strategy and typically without precision) whether we realize it

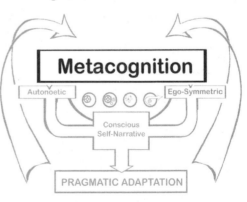

FIGURE 1.2

or not. What this tool does, in a word, is facilitate *detachment* from a problem. It allows us to step away and apart from whatever is vexing us, and by doing so to gain perspective that wouldn't be possible to attain in the direct path of the problem.[1]

The tool is metacognition, our ability to think about our thinking. We are not all on equal footing when it comes to using this tool effectively. Acquiring skill requires mental training; an inborn ability does not produce mastery. Once mastered, however, there is no more powerful internal tool available to us to solve problems, tackle challenges, and navigate paths to reach our goals.

Any time we reflect upon our thinking processes and knowledge, we are metacognizing.[2] Indeed, most of us do this all day long, though the way we do so generally lacks direction and tends to swerve into fields of endless rumination. To get the most from metacognition, we have to train ourselves to focus its power and forge the discipline necessary to stay focused despite distractions. This is a challenge, but meeting the challenge yields tangible results.

To put a finer point on all of this: metacognition is our most powerful internal tool to adjust our thinking and improve thinking outcomes.

Some of the ways this is accomplished—which we'll discuss throughout the book—include:

- Influencing feedback loops, the engines of our adaptive brains
- Addressing cognitive distortions (also known as "thinking errors")
- Catalyzing neurochemical changes in the brain

What Is a Feedback Loop?

Throughout this book, reference is made to a term we hear so frequently we seldom question what it means: "feedback loop." As it turns out, this cultural volleyball of a term is extremely important for understanding how our minds work; so important, in fact, that I think a strong argument can be made that *feedback loops are the very engines of our adaptive brains.*

One of the bankable truisms of human nature is that beneath the surface of the raging sea of complexity we experience each day, we can find a few basic governing principles that explain a great deal of why we do what we do. For roughly forty years, research across disciplines such as psychology, sociology, economics, engineering, epidemiology, and business strategy has exhaustively deconstructed and validated feedback loops as a solid governing principle with expansive explanatory power.[3] Once we get a good grasp on how they work, we'll be able to see that our brains house the most magnificent feedback loops on the planet.

Feedback loops operate in four distinct stages, each inextricably linked to the next.[3] We'll discuss each in more detail, but in short these stages, as defined by science writer Thomas Goetz, are:

1. Evidence
2. Relevance
3. Consequence
4. Action

The Evidence Stage

Every feedback loop begins with data. In the broadest sense, data can be any information that's observed, collected, measured, and stored—whether it comes from within you or without. Observing how coworkers interact at the office, seeing numbers displayed when you step on the scale, or homing in on that weird buzzing noise coming from your right front tire while driving are examples of ways we collect data.

The Relevance Stage

Here we move from data collection and storage to data input—but not data in its raw form. For data to become useful in the feedback loop, it must also be meaningful. Data that doesn't "click" is disregarded; it has to be relevant to the needs of the individual. For example, observing how your coworkers interact moves from raw data collection to meaningful data input when, perhaps, you sense that stronger integration with your peers will help you enjoy your time at work more than you do now, and maybe it will even help advance your career in the long run. That's the emotional "click" that keeps the loop moving.

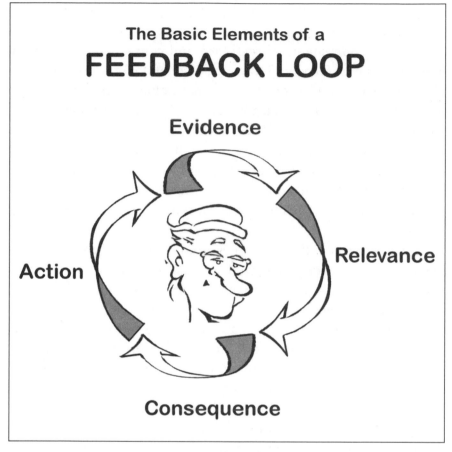

FIGURE 1.3

The Consequence Stage

Once we have meaningful data, the loop powers forward—but it won't continue unless we add another dimension: we have to know what to do with the information. You've made observations of how your coworkers interact, and you've identified an emotionally relevant reason why this information is meaningful. What's the consequence of possessing this information? Now you need to make a determination about the consequences of either doing something with the information or doing nothing—which brings us to the final stage.

The Action Stage

When the requirements of relevance and consequence have been met, we are now faced with the challenge of doing. Continuing the office scenario: you've determined that failing to better integrate with this peer group will leave you floating uncomfortably at the periphery of the office social scene. As a consequence, you may miss out on networking opportunities that could benefit your career. Your path to action is illuminated. You move definitively ahead and take steps to improve connections with members of the group to accomplish your ultimate objective of becoming a regular and important part of it.

Once action is initiated, it's measured, and new observations are made—new evidence is collected and calibrated—and the feedback loop begins anew. With each rotation of the loop, you move closer to achieving your objectives.

Given this multistage explanation, it's easy to see why feedback loops are central to countless disciplines. Engineering, for example, relies on feedback loops to plan, design, develop, and test everything from water-main pump stations to complex software applications. Business strategy relies on feedback loops to develop and launch business plans and marketing campaigns. Epidemiology relies on feedback loops to develop vaccines and new antiviral treatments. The list of examples is endless.

For our purposes, we're going to focus on what feedback loops mean in the cognitive context—we're going to remain focused on the brain. Equally important, we're going to focus on how feedback loops function as the brain's "engines." To put an even finer point on that: we're going to delve into how multiple feedback loops operating simultaneously and perpetually make our brain the incredible marvel that gets us through each day, moving us past obstacles, around threats, and ever forward toward our goals.

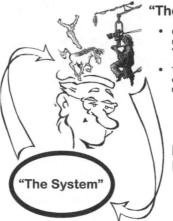

The Metacognition Loop

"The System"

- Maintains awareness of bodily states

- Motor Control (autonomic control, including heartbeat, blood pressure, etc., and voluntary motor control, including coordination of skeletal muscles for balance and action)

- Homeostasis (balance between sympathetic and parasympathetic systems)

- Sense of Self (sense of agency, bodily ownership)

- Social Emotions (empathy, norm violations, emotional processing)

"The Mental Theater"

- Creates a metacognitive representation of the "State of the System"

- This allows us to focus on specific processes via metacognitive awareness

Metacognitive Processing

- Provides new information and adjustments that can significantly change the function of specific modules within "the system."

"The System"

FIGURE 1.4

How the Human Brain "Does" Metacognition: The Metacognition Loop

Metacognition is not a mere theoretical concept—it is a function of our brains with vast neural underpinnings.[4] The brain structures that contribute to metacognition are not in any single place in the brain (as is true of most of our advanced cerebral abilities, such as memory). Rather, they communicate through neural connections in a mental network spanning multiple brain regions, particularly in the brain area known as the prefrontal cortex (PFC)—the most recently evolved part of the human brain, responsible for higher-order thinking and reasoning.[5] To simplify how the brain accomplishes metacognition, it's useful to think of a feedback loop that incorporates both conscious and unconscious components of the mind.

The System

The loop begins at what I call "The System." This is where a great deal of unconscious processing occurs via what neuroscientists refer to as "modules."[6] Imagine for a moment trying to consciously control every movement of your right hand and arm, then your left leg, and then your head tilting to the right and so forth. Thankfully we don't have to "think" about these things on a routine basis: we can deliberately decide to make these movements, but we don't have to think about *how*. A motor-function-control module within The System operates such movements automatically without the need for direct conscious effort. Constant conscious monitoring and control of such movements—to keep your balance in gravity, for example—would be impossible, never mind the need to control vital functions and organs such as your blood pressure, your lungs, your heart, your nervous system, your digestion, and almost everything else happening in your body. They all happen unconsciously within The System, the most complex processing center on the planet. However, information from The System can reach conscious awareness. Some of this information arises automatically (hence the term "automatic thoughts"—thoughts that "pop" into consciousness), but with deliberate effort some information from The System can be moved to what I call "conscious mind space." And we can delve, to an extent, into the vast modular system to make adjustments.

The Mental Theater

To understand how information from The System reaches conscious mind space, it's useful to visualize this process as images being projected onto a screen. I call this screen "the mental theater." In the mental theater, our conscious processing abilities—principally residing in the prefrontal cortex—can focus on particular states of The System (for instance, abstract modules such as social emotions or even physical modules such as blood pressure), which we may then deliberately choose to influence. In other words, information stored in The System can be retrieved or in a sense "checked out," like library books, for further inspection in the mental theater.[7]

Take, for example, certain social emotional responses you may have. Sometimes you may not understand why someone's actions strike you as, say, morally repugnant (you just "know" that they do). But if you project your emotional associations from the state of The System onto the screen of your conscious mental theater, you can take some time to figure out your reaction and perhaps come up with new insight into your thinking. Maybe you realize, for example, that the root of your moral outrage is a hazy memory of similar actions by someone in your past. Perhaps this person reminds you of a cousin who bullied you many years ago. This realization is then looped back into The System, and in this example, back into the module regulating your sense of social emotion. So the next time you encounter this person, he or she won't automatically trigger your moral indignation.[8]

At a more basic level, we can influence tangible dynamics like blood pressure through the metacognitive loop. Once we have a state of The System such as blood pressure in the theater of our mind (brought to the theater, in this case, via a feedback technology such as a blood pressure monitor, the inflatable arm cuff we're all quite familiar with), we can use any number of consciously controlled means to affect it—meditation, perhaps, or other forms of relaxation techniques. Even choosing to take medication to control your blood pressure is the result of conscious assessment. In that case, it isn't only an adjustment to thinking that's looping back into The System, but also a chemical agent that will influence The System module controlling your blood pressure.

Whether a module is emotional or physical, conscious influence is only possible through metacognitive processing—or a "conscious detachment" (which we'll discuss shortly) from whatever it is we're interested in assessing and possibly changing.

Metacognition in the Consciousness Context

OK, we've focused on the feedback loop that spans the reaches of the unconscious System and the conscious mental theater. But now we have to step back and take a wider view, because focusing *only* on the loop does not tell us the complete story of metacognition. We now have to address an exceptionally challenging problem in neuroscience—how metacognition operates within the greater context of consciousness. To work through this problem, we'll begin with a new graphic.

Back in the day, Freudians would have said that the unconscious was a seething cauldron of unfelt emotions, and the purpose of psychoanalysis was to venture with a guide into this mysterious,

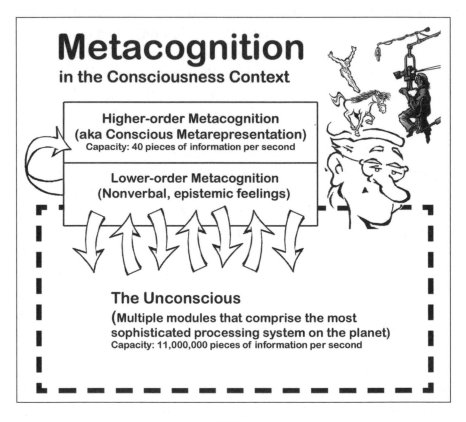

FIGURE 1.5

frightening space and track those feelings to their primal sources in childhood desires and fantasies. Today, cognitive scientists speak of the "new unconscious" to differentiate their concept from the Freudian notion of the unconscious.[9] The new unconscious isn't free from the chaos of unfelt emotions, needs, wants, and desires—but what we now understand, after more than a half a century of intense research, is that the unconscious is more akin to a massive modular processing system than to a psycho-emotional abyss. The best estimates of this system's power are that it handles roughly 11 million pieces of information per second.[10]

In contrast, the best estimate for how much information our conscious mind space can handle is about 40 pieces per second.[11] If we broke out the consciousness picture into percentages, conscious mind space would account for less than a percent of the brain's processing mojo; the rest resides in the new unconscious—a modular and unfathomably powerful mega machine.

This is where the discussion gets tricky. It's tempting to believe that we can directly access and change what's happening in the unconscious. But this is largely a misperception known as the "introspection illusion."[12] Introspection—literally "looking into oneself"—is not a waste of time, but it's also not a magical key to unlocking the unconscious. Unfortunately, many self-help and new-age books would have us believe that introspection is such a key, and that learning new (or ancient) methods of introspection will get us what we want from our unconscious minds, as if on tap.

From a science-help perspective, we have to take a more grounded view of what we can and cannot accomplish via introspection or any other inwardly focused techniques. Access to the unconscious is possible, but it is limited, and that's not a bad thing. Evolution has installed a system of inestimable value in our brains called "automaticity," which allows all of those unconscious modules we've been referring to (those and thousands more) to run without conscious intervention. Most of the thoughts and feelings we experience from our unconscious are non-verbal and "epistemic"—they're not quite tangible, but they're also not entirely abstract. These include the feelings of knowing and of forgetting; the feelings of confidence and of uncertainty; and the "tip-of-the-tongue" phenomenon (e.g., "I know the name of that rock band but it's not coming to me—but I know I know it!").

Epistemic thoughts and feelings percolate from the unconscious into a space known as "lower-order metacognition" (see the lower section of the metacognition box in figure 1.5). In this space, we begin grappling with unconscious unknowns, but they aren't yet in the theater of the mind. That doesn't happen until the command and control center—our prefrontal cortex—loops them into "higher-order metacognition" (also called "conscious metarepresentation"—the upper part of the metacognition box in the graphic). This is the part of our mind where a certain conscious clarity asserts itself—where we can mentally detach and *see* what we're thinking and feeling.

As noted, we can handle about 40 pieces of information per second in this conscious mind space. That's a sliver of what our unconscious is handling, but it's not an inconsequential amount of processing power. We can accomplish quite a lot at 40 pieces per second—and the better we become at using metacognition to our advantage, the more efficient we become at leveraging this processing power. We are, in effect, training our brains to run the metacognition loop more often and more efficiently—*and that is the essence of our brains' adaptive ability.*

Metacognitive Awareness

With the basics of metacognition laid out, let's now talk about something psychologists refer to as "metacognitive awareness" and how it fits into our exploration thus far. Psychologists use a questionnaire ranking system to determine a person's level of metacognitive awareness—*how aware we are that we're actively examining and influencing our thinking.* The more metacognitvely aware you are, the less you use autopilot to guide your thinking processes.[13]

Another way to think of metacognitive awareness is as the conscious act of coming up with strategies that select among available cognitive (thinking) responses. One researcher compared metacognitive awareness to a volume control: the higher we can raise the metacognitive volume, the more aware we are of possible thinking responses. Again, we formulate these thinking strategies in the theater of the mind—so to continue the metaphor, we're not only turning up the volume, but also the screen resolution.

Metacognitive awareness comprises four main factors:[13]

- **Metacognitive control:** The amount of conscious control we exert over our thoughts and feelings in conscious mind space
- **Metacognitive knowledge:** The quantity and quality of knowledge we're looping into conscious mind space
- **Metacognitive monitoring:** The frequency and efficiency with which we are evaluating knowledge in conscious mind space
- **Metacognitive experience:** What we learn from the knowledge in conscious mind space, and how this experience enables us to get even better at the entire process

As we learn to boost our metacognitive awareness and use it to our advantage, we gain greater influence in our brain's feedback loops. We become increasingly more self-aware about how our experiences—internal and external—influence our brains, and we find open doors to tweak those influences and, thus, change how our brains respond.

Said another way: *the better we become at thinking about our thinking, the better we become at adapting to change and choosing directions that achieve better outcomes in our lives.*

A Practical Metaphor: The Journalist Inside

My metaphor of choice for metacognition is that of the journalist, because a good journalist embodies the main characteristics of someone skilled at getting the most out of metacognitive awareness:

A good journalist . . .
- Acts quickly
- Relies on solid sources

- Asks the right questions
- Follows the story where it leads
- Doesn't gloss over inconvenient facts

(In *Part II: Do*, you'll be introduced to several other metaphors of mind—what I call the "12 Metarepresentations of Mind"—but for now we're going to stay with the journalist because it's an especially useful metaphor for metacognitive awareness.)

Here's how each of the journalist's characteristics match up with metacognitive awareness.

THE
JOURNALIST
IN YOUR MIND

FIGURE 1.6

Act quickly.

Journalists seldom have the luxury of wasting time when making determinations about how to tackle a story. To stay timely, they have to act fast. So, too, must metacognitive awareness be engaged quickly to make a difference. We have to be ready to detach and assess a situation on the spot, because the dynamics of whatever is going on are probably moving too fast for anything but immediate action.

Rely on solid sources.

Knowledge is a tool, just as logic and instinct are tools. While we can't rely on it solely (just as we cannot rely on logic or instinct solely), not making the best use of knowledge is a prescription for mediocrity, if not outright failure. My argument throughout this book is that finding and applying knowledge clues from solid sources gives us a metacognitive edge.

The sources referenced and recommended throughout this book are primarily research-based and come from a range of disciplines. A good journalist digs deep and embraces an interdisciplinary approach, because any single discipline may not offer enough information. The journalist makes it his or her mission to break down the traditional silos that too often prevent disciplines from mutually benefiting—the journalist is an interdisciplinary synthesizer of knowledge. So, too, should we rely on a breadth of sources to enhance our metacognitive awareness. Finding and digesting these sources is an ongoing learning process, one that will benefit us greatly if we make it a regular part of our routines.

Ask the right questions.

A good journalist drives to the point with incisive questions, instead of meandering around the substance of the matter with softball questions. The same is true for making best use of metacognitive awareness. We don't do ourselves any favors when we dodge and hedge instead of getting right to the core of what's going on. In addition, we don't have time for fluff; remember that time is usually not on your side in this process, so moving decisively ahead is imperative.

Follow the story where it leads.

Journalists are detectives with a penchant for expression. When they ask the right questions, the story may shift and turn, and it's their job to follow it. But they also have a sense of when not to follow, if they think they're being led down a rabbit hole. The metacognitive corollary is that there's a lot going on in your mind at any given moment. Some of it is relevant to the questions you're asking yourself, some is not. You have to train yourself to sniff out relevance and follow it if you think it will help. Anything with the odor of distraction must be disregarded.

Don't gloss over inconvenient facts.

Finally, a good journalist in possession of the facts doesn't censor out that which is inconvenient or potentially offensive. If these are the facts that matter, then they're part of the story. With metacognition you have to be willing to acknowledge everything you find, no matter how painful or embarrassing. Your internal search, like the journalist's search, has been undertaken in earnest to get to the truth, and that truth may not be pretty. That's something we all have to come to terms with.

Now, you may be asking, "Exactly how am I supposed to move through those steps if there's so little time?" The answer is that while they seem like steps, they're actually all part of a single discipline. Journalists embody each of those attributes and act on them in tandem. It's the same with metacognitive awareness. Every time we consciously engage metacognitive awareness, we don't deliberately move from point A to B to C; like a seasoned journalist, we train ourselves to do it all simultaneously.

Chapter Wrap-Up

We've discussed what metacognition is and the role it plays in our thinking; what a feedback loop is and why it's an essential concept when we're discussing the brain and mind; and how the discipline of a good journalist matches well with metacognitive awareness.

Here's a collection of Big Picture Takeaways for Chapter 1:

- Metacognition means "thinking about thinking."
- Feedback loops comprise four main elements: evidence, relevance, consequence, and action.
- The metacognition loop is the process by which unconscious information (in "The System") is looped into conscious mind space (the "mental theater") and changes to that information are ultimately looped back into The System. However, we must resist the notion that we can gain on-demand access to the unconscious through introspection; believing we can do so is called the "introspection illusion."
- We can gain a limited amount of access to the unconscious via the metacognitive loop—but it's useful to keep in mind that this process includes two levels of metacognition: lower-order

(where we receive epistemic thoughts and feelings) and higher-order (where we can *see* with a detached sense of conscious clarity what we think and feel).

- Metacognitive awareness is the degree to which we use metacognition to select from "thinking strategies" that in turn influence our thoughts and behavior.
- The disciplines embodied by a good journalist line up well with the disciplines required to use our metacognitive awareness to our greatest advantage.
- The "process steps" a journalist uses are actually not steps at all, but a continuum of thinking and action; the same goes for metacognition.
- Training ourselves to expand and improve metacognitive awareness takes effort, but doing so will improve our chances of reaching the best possible thinking outcomes.

MENTALIZATION

THE ORIGINAL MIND GAME

THERE COMES A TIME WHEN THE MIND TAKES A HIGHER PLANE OF
KNOWLEDGE BUT CAN NEVER PROVE HOW IT GOT THERE.

—Albert Einstein

W E'VE DISCUSSED METACOGNITION—what it is and how the
metacognition loop operates in our mind. Next we'll extend
the discussion to include the unique qualities of the human
brain that enhance metacognition.

Before we can do that, however, it's important to make a distinction between these abilities and the self-reflexive abilities of other species. For a long time, cognitive scientists thought that only humans could accomplish even basic self-awareness tasks, such as identifying themselves in a mirror. If you think of self-awareness as a spectrum, with relatively basic tasks such as mirror self-identification on one end and metacognitive awareness on the other, you'll have a good mental framework for what we're talking about.

As it turns out, we were wrong about at least some other species' self-awareness levels. Not only can chimpanzees and other great apes identify themselves in a mirror (as opposed to thinking their reflection is another ape), but so can dolphins, elephants, possibly macaque monkeys, and the European magpie, a relative of the crow.[1]

What humans can do that these other species cannot is detach from their self-perspective and *examine a situation that includes oneself from a position outside oneself*. For example, a chimp can easily identify itself in a mirror by pointing and tapping on the glass and noticing that the points and taps are occurring in unison with its own movements. As I mentioned, even this ability is well beyond what we thought other primates were capable of just a couple of decades ago. But the same chimp cannot assume a mental position outside the scenario in which she is identifying herself in the mirror. She cannot "metacognize" at a level removed from the present situation.

Humans, however, do this all the time without even noticing. For example, say you're in your car in heavy traffic and someone abruptly cuts you off. You immediately identify with everything that's occurring in the present scenario—yourself, the traffic, and the person cutting you off. You feel an urge to react by slamming on your horn and yelling out your window.

But evolution has provided you with a tool that can make all the difference, because you are not compelled *only* to identify with everything that is happening in the present moment. You can also mentally detach and gain perspective on what may happen next, depending on your choice of thoughts and actions. Before you slam on your horn and yell expletives out your window, you mentally step apart from what is happening and make determinations about possible outcomes of acting or not acting. In this mental space, you "see" what could happen next and decide that the potential bad outcome of acting aggressively isn't worth it, so you don't slam your horn and yell. You've effectively used your metacognitive awareness to change the situation.

After reading that last paragraph, you may ask, "Well, that's nice, but what if I get carried away by my impulse to act in the moment?" The answer is that all of us can change what happens next, although we're admittedly more inclined to react from the older part of our evolutionary inheritance—our reactive limbic system, with its well-known fight-or-flight tendencies.[2]

We'll revisit the problem highlighted by the question above throughout our exploration. Well-developed metacognitive awareness is by no means a vaccine against fight-or-flight reactions, but it is a resource that most of us do not engage consciously enough to realize its power. Metacognition is the most potent internal influence we have to alter and improve the outcomes of our brain's constellation of feedback loops, including those that operate on stout doses of adrenaline—but it takes work to make use of this influence.

So much for what we can do, self-reflexively speaking, that primates and magpies can't. What else makes our minds so special?

Theory of Mind

Theory of Mind (TOM) refers to the uniquely human ability to imagine the motives and feelings behind other people's past behavior and to predict how their behavior will unfold under their present and future circumstances. TOM has a conscious, reasoned component, but much of our "theorizing" about what others think and feel occurs via the quick and automatic processes of the unconscious. Another term for TOM is "mentalization."

Humans are the only animal whose relationships and social organization make high demands on TOM, because the breadth and depth of our societies necessitate that we "get into the heads" of others on a more or less continual basis; in other words, we're all born mentalizers.

FIGURE 2.1

That's not nearly as nefarious as it sounds. All of us, well-intentioned or not, are daily jumping in and out of others' heads, gleaning and weighing the evidence for clues to how their thinking will influence their behavior. We do this so frequently that a strong argument can be made that our mind is, in part, defined by the intersection of our thoughts with others' thoughts.

The contributions of psychologist and researcher Dr. Daniel Siegel are especially relevant here. Siegel's work, which touched off a new field, "interpersonal neurobiology," suggests that when we speak of "mind," we are speaking of interrelationships between our brain, our mind, and others' minds. In other words, mind is both internal and relational. To quote Siegel:

"The mind [is] an emergent property of the body and relationships [and] is created within internal neurophysiological processes and relational experiences. In other words, the mind is a process that emerges from the distributed nervous system extending throughout the entire body, and also from the communication patterns that occur within relationships."[3]

This is the essence of what Siegel calls "emergence": more fundamental processes—neural linkages within our brains and relational linkages between us and other people—give rise to something qualitatively new that can't be reduced back to its parts: our mind. Hence, our mind "emerges" from an ongoing internal and relational exchange. Siegel emphasizes this by saying, "The mind is embodied, not just enskulled. And the mind is also relational, not a product created in isolation."

Intentionality: Mind Mirroring Mind(s)

Hand in hand with TOM goes the notion of "intentionality," another major factor distinguishing human consciousness from that of other species. Intentionality can be thought of as the working, conscious arm of TOM and is measured in "orders" (first, second, third, and so on).

Subjects (people or other animals) capable of **first-order intentionality** are able to self-reflect about wants, needs, and desires. They can get inside their own heads. Even a chimp looking in a mirror has to do some first-order work to determine that he is looking at himself and not at another chimp, and that the grape on the floor next to "the other chimp" is actually next to him and just waiting to be picked up and devoured.

Second-order intentionality allows the subject to form a belief about another's state of mind.

At **third-order intentionality**, one can reason about what a person thinks a second person thinks.

Ascending further, **fourth-order intentionality** allows a person to reason about what a person thinks a person thinks about what another person thinks.

Only humans are capable of third- and fourth-order intentionality, and are in some cases even able to accomplish fifth- and sixth-order intentionality. Some of the complex narratives of literature are only possible using fourth-order intentionality or higher.[4]

Nonhuman primates, and possibly dolphins and pigs, are thought to be capable of first- and possibly second-order intentionality.[5]

The Role of the Inner Voice

Another distinguishing feature of the human mind is the "inner voice." The inner voice is really just a popular way of labeling metacognitive awareness in action. When we examine what's going on in our thought processes, we give a "voice" to the examiner. This voice is, of course, our own, but it's projected from a position of detachment.[6]

We have all experienced our inner voice saying "Don't do it!" or "Go for it!" How does this voice arrive at a determination to tell you to stop or go? The inner voice speaks from your metacognitive "soapbox"— that detached observer's position we've been discussing—and "voices" your internal conclusion about how to act or not act.

The question is, how educated is your inner voice? If it's informed by a well-trained process of metacognitive awareness, we can safely say that it will be a reliable source more often than not. But if the inner voice is tethered to pure instinct, absent the detachment of metacognition, following its direction could lead to trouble.

This is not an easy lesson for most of us to learn. Consumer societies often acculturate us to believe that whatever "feels good" is worth pursuing—"feels good" in this case being a proxy term for instinct. And although at times pursuing our instinctual urges will turn out just fine, at other times the results could be catastrophic.

Our instincts are heavily colored by the predicates of survival and reproduction, just as evolution ordained they would be. But when you move those same instinctual drives into complex, information-driven, consumerism-driven, technology-laden cultures, they don't fit so well. In fact, we can reasonably argue that our evolutionarily born instincts are largely out of place in the cultures our brains have created.

And that is why metacognition is such an important internal force, because it and it alone can guide both our instinctual urges and epistemic feelings in directions less at odds with circumstance.

Research has focused on the role of the inner voice in establishing a habitual inner dialogue—which is simply a psychological way to say that *what we repeat to ourselves will eventually become the "reality" we perceive ourselves to be living.* For example, if you are looking for a job and have several rejection letters sitting on your desk, your inner voice plays a pivotal role in how you'll process rejection. If your inner voice repeats that you're a failure—"Just look at all the rejections you have with not one single success!"—you'll eventually see your efforts as futile.

We can call this an "uneducated inner voice" because it's reacting from a deep well of dark emotion, not from a detached position of metacognitive awareness. From that position, your inner voice would likely send messages such as, "You can reasonably expect more failures than successes, but it only takes one solid success to change the whole game."

Probably no one described the role of the inner voice better than the great Roman emperor and Stoic philosopher, Marcus Aurelius, who said:

"Such as are your habitual thoughts, such also will be the character of your mind; for the soul is dyed by the thoughts."

Bringing It Together: The Autonoetic Personality

The first two chapters have brought us to a milestone point in the unifying graphic that started Chapter 1. Now that we understand the working parts of metacognition and mentalization, we're ready for the first big "reveal" of our exploration:

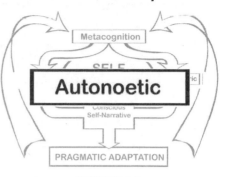

FIGURE 2.2

THROUGH EFFECTIVELY EMPLOYED METACOGNITION— ENHANCED BY MENTALIZATION—WE BECOME INCREASINGLY AUTONOETIC PERSONALITIES.

"Autonoetic" refers to the highest level of attainable self-awareness. (I use the word "attainable" only to underscore the limits of accessing the unconscious that we discussed in Chapter 1—remember, ours is a pragmatic exploration; we have to actually be able to "get there from here.")

In my definition, the autonoetic personality has very little use for autopilot when it comes to the things he or she can *consciously influence*. Autonoetic personalities understand the metacognition loop and use it to their advantage every day. They also understand how mentalization works and realize that their minds are continuously intersecting with the minds of others. They realize that they cannot control their unconscious, but via metacognition they can exert some influence on the processing modules in the vast unconscious System, and this influence can make all the difference in life outcomes. They also understand that when used efficiently, metacognition allows them to enhance their ability to direct and regulate the flow and processing of information in and out of consciousness.

Research of the last decade shows us that there are distinct benefits to becoming an autonoetic personality,[7] including:

- Higher levels of creativity
- Heightened ability to apply learned knowledge

- Enhanced adaptability in how we think about problems
- Better task performance (in our jobs, at school, etc.)

Chapter Wrap-Up

Big Picture Takeaways from Chapter 2:

- It was previously thought that only humans possessed even a marginal degree of self-awareness, but we now know that primates, dolphins, and elephants—and at least one bird species—possess rudiments of self-awareness, such as the ability to identify themselves in a mirror.
- Theory of Mind, or mentalization, refers to the uniquely human ability to speculate about others' thoughts based on their past and present behavior. This ability represents an intersection between minds, and it is this intersection that, in part, defines "mind."
- Intentionality is defined by levels or "orders," starting with first-order (basic self-awareness); second-order refers to an awareness of another's mindset; third-order refers to an awareness of another's awareness of another's mindset; and so forth. Only humans are capable of third-order and higher intentionality, possibly as high as a sixth level.
- Our "inner voice" is the popular label given to metacognitive awareness in action.
- A well-educated inner voice is trained to speak from a position of detachment, while an uneducated inner voice speaks from a position of reactive emotion.
- The first two chapters have led us to a milestone in our exploration: the autonoetic personality.[8]

PRAGMATIC ADAPTATION

CHANGING THINKING, CHANGING LIFE

TRUE LIFE IS LIVED WHEN TINY CHANGES OCCUR.

—*Leo Tolstoy*

Pragmatic Adaptation

THIS CHAPTER BEGINS with a slight detour from the discussion of metacognition into the arenas of evolutionary biology and its more recently born cousin, evolutionary psychology. At this point it's important to make a few distinctions that will color the rest of our exploration.

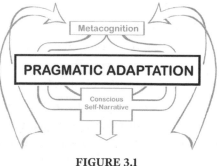

FIGURE 3.1

Most crucially, we need to develop a practical understanding of why feedback loops are so essential to what we are both as a species indebted to biological evolution, and as people continuously wrestling with the vicissitudes of cultural evolution.

Just for reference, to the right is our graphic illustrating the basic elements of a feedback loop.

As we are creatures of biological evolution, feedback loops have likely been with us since well before we emerged on the scene as *Homo erectus*. This is true of many aspects of late-stage humanity that we tend to assume are strictly "modern" in both their origins and their

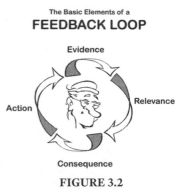

The Basic Elements of a
FEEDBACK LOOP

Evidence

Action

Relevance

Consequence

FIGURE 3.2

applications. Our bias is understandable; we can only *see* the uses and purposes of various thoughts and feelings in real time—our time.

Take *doubt*, for example. When we think of doubt, we think of a thought process we engage to challenge the veracity of an idea or assertion. Doubt would seem the tool of an advanced species, one capable of critical thought and self-reflection. But let's roll back the tape for a moment to see how this seemingly modern tool evolved as part of our cerebral toolbox. Precursors of what we call doubt have appeared along the branches of the evolutionary tree for millennia; we simply did not recognize them as such because our perception hews so closely to the here and now.[1]

Doubt in a precursor form may have been the sharp sensation that prevented an early hominid from wandering too close to the lair of a monstrous snake, lying in wait just below the surface of the sand. Would that hominid have been able to explain the sensation that saved him from becoming the serpent's dinner? Of course not, but the sensation was no less vital to his survival for lack of explanation.

The same can be argued for the components of the feedback loop. Stated another way: the reason we employ a process that leads us away from danger and toward rewards is rooted deeply in the millennia-old layers of species survival. We have evolution to thank for all of our so-called modern modes of thinking. Each of them has persisted into the present specifically because it aided in our forebearers' survival and thriving on this planet.

The other side of the story concerns the social world we live in, a world that is the product of what is frequently called "cultural evolution."[2] For most of the remainder of our exploration, we'll be moving within the corridors of cultural evolution. It is here that we will see that feedback has not only been essential to our biological survival, but is also indispensable to what I will call "pragmatic adaptation."

Adaptation that occurs within the context of biological evolution is a necessarily slow process—much too slow for us to track in anything approximating real time. Natural selection guides that kind of adaptation over the course of hundreds of thousands of years, and in some cases far longer.

Pragmatic adaptation, on the other hand, is geared toward adapting to the demands and challenges of cultural evolution, which moves extremely fast. Consider, for example, advances in medical technology related to treating cancer in just the last couple of decades. We've progressed from the trauma of imprecise treatments such as chemotherapy to loading a microRNA particle with cancer-killing agents and sending it into the body like a cruise missile aimed at a tumor.[3] That is a massive amount of progress in a short time, and we'll see even more impressive progress in the next twenty years. Or consider the massive strides made in communication, via digital social networks, smartphones, and an array of technologies that bridge distances that formerly kept people from interacting. Distance is disappearing because our brains have devised technologies that span physical gaps between people anywhere in the world.

Virtually any field or discipline produces similar stories, and they are all being written in the context of the world *our brains created*. My emphasis is meant to underscore a point that we'll return to more than once: our brains are the product of biological evolution, but that which our brains create generates the nonstop whirlwind of cultural evolution. Ironic, isn't it, that we must adapt to a world created by the most complex example of evolutionary adaptation on the planet?

Pragmatic adaptation refers to how we must adapt our thoughts and behavior to negotiate our way through the world our brains created. We do it all the time, in ways as seemingly insignificant as choosing whether to drink regular or decaffeinated coffee in the morning, and in ways that exert a major impact on our lives, such as deciding where to live, what sort of work to do, and whether we should have children.

My contention is that the most important variable in the exercise of pragmatic adaptation is feedback. Day in and day out, we make decisions based on the results of feedback loops that run in our minds without our noticing. None of us stops to think through each stage of the loop—how the data we've gathered is being processed to lead us to our next action. And yet, even without our conscious monitoring, the loops just keep moving.

There are occasions, however, when we do monitor feedback loops closely. We slow down the process, stopping each stage as if hitting "pause," to examine everything that's going on. When we're particularly concerned that something could go very wrong if we're not careful, our brain's natural threat response causes anxiety levels to increase and attention to be diverted toward the perceived threat. Taking a new job elicits this sort of response, as would deciding to get married or moving to another city.

In these cases, and countless others, successfully and pragmatically adapting to the demands of the situation is likely to have major consequences—life-altering consequences. The quality of the information in our feedback loops is of paramount importance, as is the way we handle the information. Making a mistake at the consequence stage, for example, will lead you to the wrong action path—and once you begin down that path and set off a string of effects with even more consequences, reversing course may not be easy.

The stakes are not always this high, and most of the time we process information to arrive at actions with less important outcomes. But the main point is that for outcomes big and small, we are always adapting to challenges, demands, and obstacles—and we rely on feedback to adapt successfully.

Rebooting the Adaptive Brain

Before the cognitive and behavioral sciences provided new insight into the human brain, it was conventionally assumed that the brain's capacity to change was extremely limited. Several discoveries forced a change in this assumption, most falling under the header of "brain plasticity." Brain plasticity usually refers to change at the neuro-chemical level, specifically changes in shape and size of synapses, the connection points between neurons that allow the transfer of neurotransmitters such as dopamine, serotonin, and glutamate.[4]

Not all of the brain's synapses are "plastic," but we now know that multiple brain regions are homes to neurons with synapses capable of adjusting for lesser or greater reception and projection of specific neurotransmitters. This is significant because it opens up the possibility of training the brain to do things previously thought impossible. For example, research has shown that the brain can be trained to compensate for paralysis in a limb by "rewiring" itself to control the limb through different neural pathways, and eventually it may be possible to overcome paralysis in multiple parts of the body this same way.[5]

For our purposes, we're going to zoom out from the neurochemical level (while acknowledging that it underlies everything else we'll talk about) and focus on what the brain's ability to adapt means in more pragmatic terms. We're seeking usable knowledge, and that brings us right to the possibility of change at the core of who we are.

Tenacious Adaptation Heroes: Personality Change and Well-Being

One of the last bastions of the "can't change" camp to fall was the one most central to who we are—our personality. Just in the last ten years, research has discovered that not only can our personality change, but that a change in personality can contribute more to our life satisfaction and happiness than a change in our job, our marriage, or where we live.[6] It seems that the sort of change most vital to our well-being was always overlooked in favor of obviously non-static factors—those we had the best chance of influencing. But the truth is, personality was never static; the leopard and his famous spots were always a mis-placed metaphor.

We won't spend too much time trying to understand why person-ality change was brushed aside for so long; suffice to say that this error in thinking fits a general pattern that dominated the social sciences until only recently. More central to our discussion is what we now know about personality change and how it dovetails with our explora-tion into feedback and adaptation.

First, we'll need to discuss what we mean by personality. Psychol-ogists define personality using five evaluation categories, frequently referred to as "The Big Five."[7]

The "Big Five" didn't start out with just five categories. The per-sonality theorist who started the ball rolling on personality identifica-tion, Gordon Allport, posited that there were 4,504 adjectives that

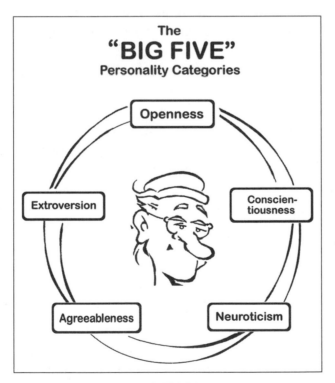

FIGURE 3.3

could be used to describe specific personality traits. He arranged these thousands of traits into three overarching categories:

1. **Cardinal traits** that dominate a person's mindset and outlook
2. **Central traits** that influence a person's behavior
3. **Secondary traits** that only appear under certain situations

That many traits were too confusing and unwieldy for most people to find useful, so eventually another theorist, Raymond Cattell, used a statistical technique to reduce Allport's enormous list to 171 terms. He later refined the list into a 16-personality-factor model. Eventually two more personality theorists, Paul Costa, Jr., and Robert McCrae, refined the 16-factor model even further, winnowing it down to five key personality categories—what we now know as "The Big Five."[8]

A person is evaluated in each personality category via a question-naire and assigned a numerical score; the higher the score in a given category, the more of that Big Five trait the person has in his or her personality. While not perfect, this assessment has been well validated and does provide a general means to predict how someone will react to another person, thing, idea, or occurrence.[9]

For example, we can safely predict that an individual who scores high on "Openness to Experience" will be more receptive to new and challenging ideas than someone who scores low in this category. Someone who scores high in "Conscientiousness" likely spends more time getting organized than a person who scores low in this category. Someone who scores high in "Extroversion" will be more gregarious and expressive than someone who scores low in this category.

Previously, it was thought that a person's score in any category was fixed—probably since his or her early adolescence.[10] The most recent research shows, however, that we can change in any category, and depending on our environments, we may find ourselves changing through adaptation without even noticing.

Does that mean we can exhaustively change who we are? No, because each of us will encounter varying levels of change resistance in different categories, which influences the degree to which change can be achieved. And, for reasons we don't yet entirely understand, some people are more change-resistant than others. There will always be parameters of the self—particular traits that are indicative of *you* no matter what.

Exhaustive change aside, most of us can change our personalities in significant ways, and doing so can result in a more beneficial outcome than straining to change external factors. How does personality change occur? Via a term we've discussed and will continue to discuss: pragmatic adaptation. *We must first identify our limitations in any given personality category, and then pragmatically adapt to address these limitations.*

In fact, research has shown that personality change is as essential a variable in life satisfaction as socioeconomic factors (income, employment or unemployment, and marital status). And personality change is twice as important to life satisfaction as all of the major demographic variables (where we live, how many kids we have, and so on) combined.[11]

Similar studies reveal that we'd do well to spend more time thinking about our Big Five than about external variables we can't always control. Even when we can control them—as in the case of, say, choosing to relocate—such changes don't address the core of our well-being unless we also tackle personality change. The problem is, whether or not we choose to regard personality as a variable, we take it with us, so we're far better off keeping it foremost in mind. An ancient adage bears mentioning: "Wherever you go, there you are."

Major Points on the Adaptation Raceway: Allostasis and Homeostasis

Two simultaneously complementary and contrary terms say an awful lot about how the human brain manages to adapt to an ever-changing world, and they directly influence our personality repertoire: *allostasis* and *homeostasis*. Let's take homeostasis first.

Homeostasis refers to the tendency of a system to maintain a stable, balanced condition instead of bounding from one extreme to another. The renowned physiologist Walter Bradford Cannon coined the term with respect to physical systems—and, as we know, the brain is such a system. In fact, our brains and our bodies in total are a physical system, and as such they tend toward homeostasis—the "comfort zone" of stability and equilibrium.[12]

Allostasis, in contrast and complement, is the necessity of a system to adapt to ever-changing internal and external environments in order to get closer to the holy grail of homeostasis.[13]

Our brains embody both of these dynamics. For example, our brains seek homeostatic balance between our sympathetic and parasympathetic nervous systems—between the softly focused resting state and the stress-alert, fight-or-flight state—but we never remain only in one or the other. Instead, our brains toggle between these

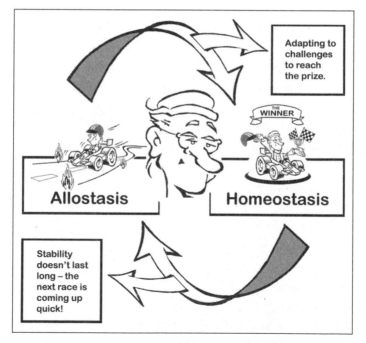

FIGURE 3.4

states in response to internal and external influences. If we remain in either for too long, there are psychological and physical consequences. A prolonged period of resting state could contribute to the onset of depression. Or the hyper-stress response to an ongoing fight-or-flight state could lead to a spike in blood pressure. (Imagine how your car would respond if you tried to start it after it had been in the garage for a year; or imagine the effects on your engine if you red-lined it on the highway for hours on end.) Neither state is healthy in extended doses.

Which is why, as a matter of day-to-day functioning, our brains are also allostatic, constantly adapting to challenges, obstacles, twists, and turns arising from within and without. A prime example of frequent allostatic adaptation is how we handle what cognitive psychologists call "thinking errors."[14]

Dealing with Thinking Distortions

One of the many contributions of Cognitive Behavioral Therapy (CBT)—a therapeutic technique that focuses on changing emotional responses by changing thinking—to understanding and managing how we process and adapt to our thoughts and emotions has been to identify a litany of "thinking errors" that erroneously filter information, no matter its source. When we indulge thinking errors, our brains misinterpret information (evidence), resulting in a distortion of feedback loops—and this, in turn, hampers our ability to adapt.

Common thinking errors:
- All-or-nothing thinking
- Overgeneralization
- Disqualifying the positive
- Disqualifying the negative
- Mind reading
- Fortune telling
- Magnification and minimization
- Emotional reasoning

- Labeling
- Personalizing
- Faulty comparisons
- False expectations

All-or-nothing thinking: Thinking in terms of absolutes; it is either one way or another with no middle ground possible. "If someone has acted coldly toward me in the past, that person will always act that way toward me in the future." "I won't settle for anything less than the specific promotion I want, and if I don't get it, I'll quit—it's all or nothing."

Overgeneralization: Using one perceived aspect of something or someone to describe everything or everyone that is similar. "People who buy huge SUVs aren't conscious of the environment. Anyone who gets a tattoo must be rebellious."

Disqualifying the positive: Thinking that if something good happens it's by luck or accident, but when something bad happens it was the expected outcome. "If I do well on this test it'll be a fluke, but if I do poorly it'll be because I'm not smart enough."

Disqualifying the negative: Thinking that if something bad happens it won't reflect anything about you, but if something good happens it will be because of your actions. "If I don't get this job, I know it'll be because I'm too intimidating for the hiring committee; they'll want someone who they can walk all over instead."

Mind reading: Thinking that you're able to correctly determine what someone else is thinking even if you have little or no evidence. "My boss expects me to ask for a raise, so I know she's going to be defensive when I speak to her."

Fortune telling: Predicting the worst possible outcome for any given situation. "I'll go on the date, but it's really useless because I already know the relationship won't go anywhere."

Magnification and minimization: Either overstating or understating the reality of a situation without considering contrary evidence. "If I get turned down by Stephanie, it'll prove that I am truly worthless and undeserving of anyone's attention."

Emotional reasoning: Believing your negative feelings without questioning them and acting accordingly. "I feel angry so my anger must be justified."

Labeling: Placing a label on a person that colors the rest of your thinking regardless of contrary evidence. "John is wearing two earrings, so I know he's not someone I can take seriously."

Personalizing: Thinking that any event, no matter how innocuous, has something to do with you. "Sarah didn't smile when she saw me in the hall today at work, so she must be upset with me."

Faulty comparisons: Failing to see important distinctions between people or things, or acting as if differences don't matter. "A manager at one big company is just as miserable as a manager at another; it's the same everywhere."

False expectations: Failing to see the true dimensions, variables, or possibilities of any given goal or problem. "If I get a degree, I'll get a job that pays a lot of money—that's just how it works."

Examples of Thinking Errors Distorting Feedback Loops

Since feedback loops depend on the inputting and processing of evidence, they can be distorted by thinking errors. An inaccurate mental filter fostered by a thinking error can alter every other step in the thinking process.

For example, if you begin by thinking that either you're going to accomplish 100 percent of your goal or none of it, and no other outcome is acceptable, you're going to be far too dogmatic at the consequence stage because you've already determined that there's no reason to move ahead unless you can get everything you want.

Rarely is this possible, and starting with an all-or-nothing stance will cause you to ignore the possibility that achieving part of your goal now may set you up for achieving more of it later. You've limited your options with a thinking error you probably don't even realize you're committing.

If you begin with the thinking error of "mind reading," you are likely to process the evidence with a skewed perspective based on the false belief that you can know with any degree of certainty what someone else is thinking. If you begin with "faulty expectations," then you're likely to misjudge evidence and either under- or overestimate the resources required to advance toward action.

To get the most from feedback loops, you'd do well to identify your thinking errors and check yourself as soon as you start engaging in one or more of them. Very often we engage in more than one at a time; overgeneralization and all-or-nothing thinking, for example, tend to appear together.

Thinking Errors and Automatic Thoughts

Thinking errors are difficult to identify and check before they do their damage because their source material—automatic thoughts—have been "bubbling up" from our unconscious for most of our lives. (Remember the term "epistemic" from Chapter 1? Some percolation from the unconscious is useful, and some of it is downright negative and erroneous.) Each of us is more susceptible to certain errors than others, but all of us fall prey to erroneous automatic thoughts to some degree every day.

Indulging thinking errors for years establishes neural patterns in our brains. We find ourselves naturally falling into the tracks of mind reading, or labeling, or emotional reasoning, because in a very real sense those tracks are physical structures that have developed in our brains over time and we are "trained" to follow them. Seen this way, thinking errors are not really thoughts at all, but habitual actions we take once a misleading automatic thought has entered our conscious mind space and grabbed our attention.[15]

This is where our discussion of metacognition and the unconscious back in Chapter 1 is useful to revisit, particularly with respect to epistemic feelings and thoughts. Take a look at Figure 3.5 illustrating this point again for reference.

Our brains are constantly producing automatic thoughts—whether negative or not. The truth is, we don't fully understand why the unconscious produces a seemingly endless chatter of information, but we do know that it happens perpetually, and our ability to manage these thoughts is essential to adaptation.

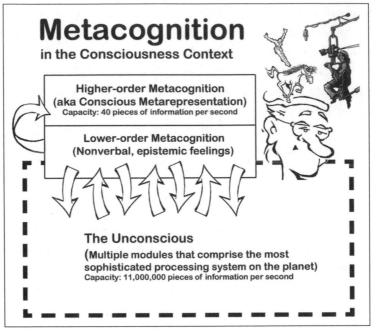

FIGURE 3.5

Using the Tools of Attention and Problem Solving to Help Our Cause

We know that we cannot stop the surge of automatic thoughts from our subconscious, but what we can do is train ourselves to focus our attention constructively. Cognitive Behavioral Therapy can help us accomplish this by offering ways to enact the discipline of problem solving.

Problem-solving rules from CBT

1. Only focus your attention on problems you can solve; don't get caught up in the endless loop of focusing on problems clearly outside your influence.
2. Focus your attention on one problem at a time, and do so in earnest.
3. Focus on self-change, not on changing others.

4. Consider not doing anything as one option.
5. Remember, you are not your thoughts.

Remembering that you are not your thoughts is the crucial rule that guides us through the others. Your brain will never stop filling your conscious mind space with thoughts, *but those thoughts do not define you.* They are the natural outcome of a normally functioning brain. How we handle those thoughts is the real issue, and that's where problem solving comes into play.[16]

In a sense, every feedback loop is engaged to solve a problem. Dieting, for example, is about solving the problem of losing excess weight (and improving health, looking better, etc.). Working harder on the job is about solving the problem of bridging the gap from your current position to the next level. Improving communication with your significant other helps you identify the obstacles that prevent you from enjoying a more fulfilling relationship, and so forth.

In tandem with being aware of thinking errors, we can use the rules from CBT to keep us on track in addressing them. (Consider this a brief preview of the tools we'll be delving into in *Part II: Do.*)

Why Problems Seem to Come in Groups

"When it rains, it pours" is a familiar saying that means when one thing goes wrong, other things are sure to go wrong as well. Similarly, "problems always come in threes."

These sayings have a certain gut wisdom that all of us, whether we like it or not, are in touch with, though it's rarely clear why trouble seems to come all at once. Feedback loops can provide some insight into this unpleasant reality.

It's not necessarily that multiple external problems are "happening" to you all at once, but quite possibly that you've wandered into a patch of difficult-to-manage thinking distortions that have skewed your view of what's going on in your life.

Here's the good news: everything you've been learning so far in Part I enables healthy detachment from those distortions, and once

you become a master of detachment, you reach another crucial rev-
elation in our exploration—you become "ego-symmetric."

Striking a Balance

The term "ego-symmetric" strikes a judicious balance between two
poles that relate to your self-concept: ego-syntonic and ego-dystonic.
When you function in an ego-syntonic manner, you believe that the
ongoing stream of thoughts surfacing in your consciousness truly represent *who you are* ("syntonic" literally means *attuned* and "ego" is
simply shorthand for *self*).

When you function in an ego-dystonic manner you find that the
waves of percolating thoughts do not agree ("dystonic" meaning *poorly attuned*) with who you are. In this mode, you are prone to reject
these thoughts—be they wants, desires, impulses, or other—as unrep-
resentative of the "you" you believe yourself to be, or want to be.

Another way to think of these poles is with two simple statements
that the inner voice speaks from the cerebral soapbox:

1. "This is truly me."
2. "This is not truly me."

No one operates at either pole exclusively. Our reactions to
thoughts are often case-specific. For example, if you're inexpe-
rienced with public presentations you may, when confronted
with the challenge of making one, find yourself awash in thoughts
that convince you that it's a terrifying prospect and it will likely
result in deep embarrassment. The fear associated with speaking
in front of a group produces an ego-syntonic reaction. You perceive the terrifying thoughts as accurate because they represent
the "true" you. In practice, the thoughts may be entirely inaccurate, but what matters in the moments of self-evaluation is how
the thoughts *feel*. If they feel true, and if they continue to hold
sway over consciousness, your behavior will fall in alignment with
those thoughts.

On the other hand, perhaps you are tired of being ruled by fearful thoughts, and when presented with an opportunity to make a presentation, you confront these thoughts and declare them (within the corridors of your mind) to be unaligned with who you want to be. In this case, the reaction to the barrage of terrifying thoughts is ego-dystonic. They do not tell the right story about your ideal self—the self you strive to become.

In the example I just gave, most people say that the correct pole is ego-dystonic, and I would agree. But the central issue is a bit hidden. If we deconstruct the thought-evaluation process that moved your thoughts to the ego-dystonic, we'll see that there had to be a few crucial moments of detachment during which the percolating negative thoughts were paused and reviewed. It's in this space that metacognition happened and the outcome changed.

When you automatically jump to a pole—whether ego-syntonic or ego-dystonic—you aren't thinking about thinking; you're simply defaulting. Defaulting is always the easier way to go. Pausing, evaluating, and challenging are bricks in a much more challenging road—but only by taking that road can we hope to achieve balance between the poles. Without balance, automatic thoughts push us around and we default to escape the discomfort.

The "balance" is achieved via healthy detachment from these thoughts and determining whether they are truly telling the right story. The answer doesn't live at either pole, but in the symmetry between them—the metacognitive space.

Bringing it Together: The Ego-Symmetric Personality

Much of this chapter has dealt with the emotional part of our mindscape. As we've discussed, cognitive psychology has developed useful tools for affecting our emotional states by influencing our thinking. Earlier in the book, the role

FIGURE 3.6

of metacognition was presented as the major tool (you might call it the "rubric tool" in that it presides over all the others) for influencing our thinking process, and this in turn has a direct effect on emotional outcomes.

These discussions bring us to another milestone in our exploration: becoming more *ego-symmetric* as a means to successfully adapt to the range of internal and external influences barraging us each day.

> **THE EGO-SYMMETRIC PERSONALITY IS ABLE TO DETACH FROM NEGATIVE AND ERRONEOUS INFORMATION THAT, IF INDULGED, WOULD UNDERMINE THE SELF'S ABILITY TO ACHIEVE ITS GOALS. BEING EGO-SYMMETRIC IS NOT THE SAME AS BEING "COLD" AND UNEMOTIONAL— INSTEAD, IT'S ABOUT BEING IN BETTER CONTROL OF HOW NEGATIVITY AFFECTS OUR ABILITY TO ADAPT AND THRIVE.**

Chapter Wrap-Up

In this chapter we discussed feedback loops, pragmatic adaptation, the brain's adaptive capabilities, and the reality of personality change. Below are the Big Picture Takeaways from Chapter 3.

- Feedback loops have four distinct stages, each linked to the next: (1) Evidence, (2) Relevance, (3) Consequence, and (4) Action.
- We rely on feedback loops all the time for matters big and small, even though they usually process information without our noticing.
- Feedback is the key to pragmatic adaptation—the corollary to biological adaptation—defined as the process of adapting to the challenges, threats, and demands of the world our brains created.
- Pragmatic adaptation is central to success in an extremely fast-paced world driven by the relentless force of cultural evolution.
- Research in brain plasticity has shown that the brain is much more flexible than previously thought.

- Not only is the brain flexible in the neurochemical sense, but also at the level of personality; this assertion was not given much credence even twenty years ago.
- Personality change is more important to well-being than external socioeconomic and demographic variables.
- Allostasis and homeostasis are both crucial points to understand when trying to make sense of our brains' ability to adapt.
- Thinking errors—often the product of erroneous information percolating from the unconscious—can distort feedback loops and hamper our ability to adapt.
- We've reached another milestone in our exploration: the ego-symmetric personality.

TRACING THE NARRATIVE THREAD

THE POWER OF SCRIPTING AND SALIENCE

"WE CONSTRUCT A NARRATIVE FOR OURSELVES, AND THAT'S THE THREAD THAT WE FOLLOW FROM ONE DAY TO THE NEXT. PEOPLE WHO DISINTEGRATE AS PERSONALITIES ARE THE ONES WHO LOSE THAT THREAD."

— *Paul Auster*

L ET'S SURVEY our exploration so far. We've discussed feedback loops as the engines of our adaptive brains, and looked closely at the four stages of a feedback loop—evidence, relevance, consequence, and action. We focused on how these stages are applicable in the cognitive context.

We discussed feedback's role in pragmatic adaptation—the means by which we adapt to the flux and pulsation of cultural evolution. Cultural evolution, we said, is the product of our brains—which, ironically, are the product of millennia of biological evolution, a dynamic that moves far more slowly than cultural evolution. To successfully adapt to the demands of cultural evolution, we must have access to feedback; it's the very key to our pragmatic forward progress.

We also spent some time discussing the marvels of our adaptive brains, specifically the ability to change elements of our personalities that were previously thought unchangeable. We now know that personality change is central to our well-being, and that it outweighs an array of external factors, including marital status, employment, and where we choose to live.

In our earlier exploration of metacognition, we spoke of something psychologists call "metacognitive awareness." The more metacognitively aware we are, the greater the degree of influence we have over our thoughts and behavior. More to the point, a higher degree of metacognitive awareness provides us with prime opportunities to affect our brain's constellation of feedback loops.

We learned that metacognition is not a mere theoretical concept, but a neural reality—a physical dimension of our brains. Our metacognitive abilities are distinguished from the self-awareness of other species by our ability to mentally detach from the immediate situation to observe our thinking, as if from a position outside ourselves. Other animals, such as chimps and elephants, can identify themselves in a mirror by tracing their movements and discovering that what they see is, in fact, not another creature but themselves pointing and tapping the glass. But they are unable to detach from that scenario and observe themselves thinking through the process of identifying themselves in the reflection. This higher-order level of detachment is, as far as we know, unique to humans, and it provides us with tremendous capabilities that we often take for granted.

We spoke briefly about the journalist as a metaphor for metacognitive awareness, because each of the disciplines embodied by a good journalist is crucial to the effective practice of metacognitive: 1) acting quickly, 2) relying on solid sources, 3) asking the right questions, 4) following the story where it leads, and 5) not glossing over inconvenient facts.

We also explored the role of the inner voice as our internal verbal barometer for metacognitive awareness in action. The crucial question, we said, is whether the inner voice is speaking from a metacognitive "soapbox," or if it lacks the detachment of metacognition and is speaking from instinct and untethered emotion. We made the distinction between an "educated" and an "uneducated" inner voice, and emphasized the need to educate our inner voice to lead us to better outcomes in our lives.

With that part of our exploration as backdrop, we are now going to discuss how all of this leads us to begin tracing the thread that holds all of it together, and will lead us to a point in our exploration called conscious self-narrative.

Here again is the unifying graphic from Chapter 1. Before you move on, note the points that have been previously touched upon. This is just an interim refresher. Chapter 5, the final chapter in Part I, will capture these points again more holistically.

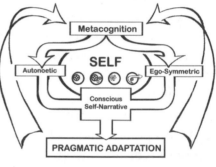

FIGURE 4.1

Tracing the Narrative Thread

The term "narrative thread" has been used by philosophers, psychologists, and novelists—among others—to describe essentially the same thing: how we hold our "selves" together in a more or less unified way as we proceed through our lives. The use of "selves," in quotation marks, instead of "self" is intentional, because more and more research indicates that the "I," or self-identity, in our minds is not one coherent entity, but a composite of interplaying self-identities. At times this interplay is erratic, at other times in sync—but the crucial point is that the unified "I" within is a useful illusion that our brains foster on our behalf.

Why, from an adaptation standpoint, is this illusion so important? Without a unifying self-narrative (what philosopher Daniel Dennett calls the "Center of narrative gravity,"[1]) we would lack an internal centering mechanism to come back to as we address the situations and challenges of the day. You might think of this as similar to a base runner in a baseball game having to "touch base" before running to the next base. Our brains developed this centering mechanism to keep us focused on our prime evolutionary objectives: to avoid threats and pursue rewards. Even though we present a somewhat different "self" in any given situation (e.g., the "self" you present at the office versus the "self" you present at a party), our brains make sure that we always "touch base" to regain the narrative centering that holds our personalities together.

We can observe how important this adaptive mechanism is by studying schizophrenics—those whose brains are unable to draw the narrative "threads" together to regain the unified sense of self most of us possess. In this case, the "threads" are flailing in disparate directions, failing to find the central harnessing point that would pull them into a coherent self-identity.

At this point, you may be asking, "OK, so which is it? Are we just composites of multiple 'selves,' or are we one 'self' with different ways of interacting with the world?" At the risk of sounding glib, the answer is, "Yes." The best evidence uncovered by cognitive science so far suggests that we are not just one "self"—we are composite "selves"—but our brains adaptively foster a unified sense of self (the "I" within the "You") because that is the most effective means to survive and thrive in this world. The important takeaway is that each of us with a well-functioning brain lives our life with a narrative thread that keeps us centered—keeps us "touching base"—and allows us to avoid being subsumed by the chaos of multiple "selves" trying to find their place in the world.

Internalizing Narrative Scripts

The term "script" often suggests a stack of papers that an actor refers to before delivering her lines on stage. That's actually not a bad metaphor for something we'll simply call "external scripting," in contrast to the internal scripts each of us continuously refers to in our mind as we process the events of the day.

External scripting comes to us from sources of external influence—our employers, peers, parents, government, churches, etc. We're exposed to this variety of scripting every day, and we internalize the scripts given to us by these sources for a multitude of reasons. For example, we internalize our employer's scripting because our jobs depend on it. We internalize our peers' scripting because we value their perception of us and don't want to jeopardize our standing in the group. We internalize our churches' scripting because we believe that it is passed through the church to us from a higher power that we want to please.

External scripting contributes to the running scripts we refer to on a daily basis, which are a combination of external influence (much of which we have already internalized) and genetic propensity. For example, the external scripting from our employer may direct us to be more extroverted in our interactions with coworkers and clients, but that scripting must meld with our genetic propensity to be an introvert. Which will win out? Well…both, and neither. Instead of either script "winning," we pragmatically adapt to the needs of the situation and alter our genetically scripted style (what psychologists refer to as our "natural style").[2] If, of course, we fail to pragmatically adapt, then we likely fail to accomplish the objective in front of us.

What makes external scripting such an important "moving part" is not that it automatically alters how we handle whatever life throws our way—because the truth is, much of the time it doesn't. The fact that our employer wants us to become more extroverted doesn't mean that we'll pragmatically adapt to meet that demand. Perhaps we will, but perhaps we won't. Perhaps, instead, the true meaning of pragmatically adapting in this case is to realize that we are in the wrong job. That may sound extreme, but think of how often we try to cram ourselves into a "scripted" situation that just doesn't work for us. Consider, for example, the person who values authenticity and straightforward dealing, but works for an organization that only pays lip service to those values. If we force-adapt to those situations over and over again, we'll eventually burn out. Aside from the psychological toll this takes, it could result in losing the job anyway.

The same goes for any number of life scenarios where an external script that radically counters our natural style is placed in front of us. We try to internalize it, but making it "fit" is tedious, if not torturous.

Most of us will wrestle with trying to make it work anyway, sometimes for years. Whom are we helping? We might say we're helping our family by keeping a job that's pure agony, but when you go home at night emotionally spent, with nothing left to give your family—are they truly benefiting? That's just one example of many, but the main point remains the same: sometimes pragmatically adapting does not mean finding a way to meld an external script with our natural style; sometimes it means adapting by finding an entirely different role that more closely fits who we are and what we have to offer. That's what makes identifying external scripts so important—seeing them clearly can provide the impetus for making better decisions. Seeing the script for what it is—good or bad—shows us ways in which adaptation is necessary to live a more fulfilled life.

Narrative Salience

The term "salience" in neuroscience refers to something notably distinct from everything else that draws our attention and catalyzes focus.[3] Salience plays an integral role in self-narrative, because it serves as the cognitive lodestone that keeps us centered.

For example, let's say you have just moved to a new city and are just starting to find your way around town, learn the streets and major milestones, and become acquainted with the people living near you. In this brand-new environment, do you become a "brand-new you"? Another way to ask that question is, if everything in this new place is entirely new to you—distinct in every way from anywhere else you've lived—do you change to suit the newness of this place?

The answer, of course, is that you do not. Instead, you integrate the newness of the place into your existing self-narrative. What allows you to pull that off without becoming lost (*lost* psychologically, not geographically)? Evolution has taken care of that for you. Your brain is already identifying salient aspects of this place and integrating them into existing neural networks. In other words—your self-narrative is being modified without losing its "thread" by a potent evolutionary force that every well-functioning brain uses to adapt.[4]

In this way, our self-narratives are always changing in subtle or substantial ways. Narrative is never static. And, as we have discussed in previous chapters, our brains are never static. Our personalities are never static. We are forever in a state of flux, however imperceptible this may be to us from hour to hour. And this, I want to take a moment to remind you, is a very good thing—not a force to fear, but one to embrace as the very spirit of our being human.

Back to Feedback

In Chapter 1 we explored feedback loops as the engines of the adaptive brain, and at this point it's appropriate to tie that understanding to the role of self-narrative and the potency of salience.

If you think of the ongoing procession of feedback loops in your brain—running every waking moment of every day—then you already have a model for self-narrative. We are simply using different semantic methods of referring to the same dynamics. Why is it important that we do so? Quite simply because speaking only of the brain's constellation of ongoing feedback loops is too mechanistic a way to describe something so multidimensional—overflowing with nuance and subtleties. The crucial term, no matter what framework of meaning we use, is "adaptation."

Note that the purpose of using metacognition to influence our brains' feedback loops is to enhance an adaptive response to whatever challenges, obstacles, and objectives we face or attempt to achieve.

Also note that our self-narrative is an ever-changing flow integrating external scripting and salience—which is also an adaptive process.

We have reached a point in our exploration where the contexts overlap—providing us with an enriched understanding of our topic. Whether we use the mechanistic terminology of feedback loops or the metaphorical terminology of self-narrative, we have arrived at what physicists call a "principal vector."

Bringing it Together: Conscious Self-Narrative

We've reached another milestone in our exploration, and this—above all the others—is the easiest to grasp, because everything leading up to this point has already made it self-evident.

FIGURE 4.2

WHEN WE EFFECTIVELY USE METACOGNITION TO INFLUENCE FEEDBACK LOOPS, WE CONSCIOUSLY INFLUENCE OUR SELF-NARRATIVE, AND WE FOSTER A GREATER ABILITY TO PRAGMATICALLY ADAPT. WE ARE NOT RIDING THE WAVES OF HAPPENSTANCE—WE ARE USING THE ADAPTIVE POWER OF OUR BRAINS TO DIRECT OUR PATHS TO THE ABSOLUTE BEST OF OUR ABILITIES. WE ARE, IN A SENSE, ACTIVELY WRITING OUR NARRATIVE INSTEAD OF WATCHING IT BEING WRITTEN FOR US WHILE WE CRUISE ON AUTOPILOT.

Chapter Wrap-Up

Big Picture Takeaways from Chapter 4:

- The term "narrative thread" has been used by philosophers, psychologists, and novelists—among others—to describe essentially the same thing: how we hold our "selves" together in a more or less unified way as we proceed through our lives.

- The fact that we experience ourselves as an "I" and not a "We" is evidence of how essential the narrative thread is, even though we seldom realize it is because being an "I" comes so naturally.
- Narrative scripts are both internal and external, and they exert great influence on us daily—usually without conscious assessment. They "run" below the surface of consciousness.
- Salience plays an integral role in self-narrative because it serves as the cognitive lodestone that keeps us centered.
- Narrative is never static. Our brains are never static. Our personalities are never static. We are forever in a state of flux, however imperceptible this may be to us from hour to hour.
- We've reached another milestone in our exploration, and it's a big one: conscious self-narrative.

THE MINDSCAPE

LOOPING IT ALL TOGETHER

EVERY NOW AND THEN A MAN'S MIND IS STRETCHED BY A NEW IDEA OR
SENSATION, AND NEVER SHRINKS BACK TO ITS FORMER DIMENSIONS.

—*Oliver Wendell Holmes Sr.*

W E CONCLUDE *Part I: Know* where we started it, with our unifying graphic. Now it's time to survey the map of the mindscape
we've just explored, retracing our steps to solidify understandings before moving forward. Instead of rehashing, let's take a slight-
ly different approach and watch a hypothetical interview between
a reporter and an explorer. The reporter wants to know the who's,
why's, and what's of the exploration. The explorer, having just completed the first major stretch of the trek, is more than happy to oblige.

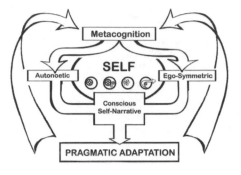

FIGURE 5.1

REPORTER: OK, give us some context. Where did this all begin?

EXPLORER: We started at the top, so to speak—with metacognition, which literally means "thinking about thinking."

REPORTER: Is that anything like what the philosopher Albert Camus meant when he said, "An intellectual is someone whose mind watches itself"?[1]

EXPLORER: Yes, I suppose so, but I think in this case we can swap out the word "intellectual" with "a good thinker," because that's really closer to what we're talking about. Understanding metacognition is about becoming a better thinker.

REPORTER: Please elaborate. I mean, we're all "thinkers" aren't we? How does someone become a "better thinker"? Are you talking about becoming smarter?

EXPLORER: You could use a term like "smarter," but that's also too narrow. When I say we want to become better thinkers, I mean that we want to learn to make better use of our brains' abilities in order to improve how we address problems, challenges, obstacles, and all of the things that arise when we're trying to achieve something worthwhile.

REPORTER: Worthwhile like what?

EXPLORER: Like living a more fulfilling life.

REPORTER: You're saying that making better use of metacognition is a means to improve our thinking, and that can lead to a more fulfilling life?

EXPLORER: Nicely said. Yes, I am saying exactly that. But of course there's much more to the process than just a summary statement.

REPORTER: For example?

EXPLORER: Well, one of the biggest moving parts along the way is understanding what you might call the "engines of our adaptive brains," feedback loops. Our brains operate much like a modular processing system, and it's useful to envision that system running via a vast constellation of feedback loops. Information (you could also call it "evidence") is inputted and evaluated for its relevance. If relevant, then another evaluation happens to determine the consequence of acting or not acting on the information. If a determination to act is made, then action occurs.

REPORTER: And then?

EXPLORER: And then the outcomes of the action are fed back into the feedback loop as new evidence, and so forth.

REPORTER: Interesting, but how does that link up with metacognition?

EXPLORER: Excellent question! Metacognition is our most powerful internal tool for influencing feedback loops. Said another way, our brains are equipped with a remarkable ability to mentally detach from what you could call the immediacy of our thinking, and that ability allows us to exert a certain amount of influence over the processing of feedback loops.

REPORTER: Are you saying that we can use metacognition to completely control our brains?

EXPLORER: Actually, no, although that's a popular misconception sometimes called the "introspection illusion." I'm saying we can use metacognition to exert more *conscious control* on our thinking. The distinction here is really important because most of our brain's processing doesn't occur in what we call "conscious mind space." It happens in a vast unconscious System. We can't just change whatever we want whenever we want in The System, and believe it or not, that's a good thing.

REPORTER: Why? It sounds like it would be useful to take control of what's happening in the unconscious.

EXPLORER: Well, imagine if you could turn off the unconscious processing module that controls your motor functions and take over the controls with conscious reasoning. You'd then have to consciously control all of your muscle movements, not to mention respond to every nervous-system signal throughout your body, and do things like keep your heart pumping, your lungs working, and your digestive system functioning. You would have to do all of that by thinking about it.

REPORTER: Sounds impossible.

EXPLORER: It is, which is why it's far better that we allow our unconscious to handle it. That's just one example out of thousands. Our unconscious processes about 11 million pieces of information every second.

REPORTER: OK, so what about conscious mind space? What can we do there?

EXPLORER: Best estimates are that we can process about 40 pieces of information per second consciously. While that sounds infinitesimal compared to the unconscious (and it is), it's an adequate amount of processing power to exert a certain amount of influence on the feedback loops. We cannot, however, expect to jump in and get control of the unconscious on tap. Evolution didn't provide us with that ability, and for good reason.

REPORTER: All right, give me an example of something we *can* do consciously.

EXPLORER: Well, the main reason we want to enhance our metacognitive awareness is to improve the flow of information in and out of conscious mind space, and exert more control over it while it's in conscious mind space.

Here's an example: Let's say that you're having a hard time figuring out why you doubt yourself so much. You might call this a self-image problem, and it makes establishing and trying to achieve new goals really difficult. Almost every day doubtful thoughts pop into your consciousness, and you find yourself reacting to them emotionally. You feel bad about yourself, and the worse you feel, the more depressed you become about doing anything worthwhile.

What you don't realize is that you're in a negative-thinking feedback loop that you are actually reinforcing all the time. You don't realize this because you are "in" the problem. You need to use your brain's ability to detach from the problem to examine the negative-thought feedback loop from outside the emotionally fueled surge of the loop. From this position, you can consciously assess what's going on, and instead of ruminating about all the negatives, you can shift to a role of strategic analyst and determine what needs to happen to change the feedback loop.

REPORTER: Intriguing, but that sounds a little mechanistic, no?

EXPLORER: In a sense it is mechanistic, because our brains and bodies are, in a manner of speaking, organic machines. But that's just a metaphor for understanding ourselves—it's not a concrete, absolute definition. Another metaphor is "self-narrative." This process is just as easily explained by thinking of yourself consciously changing the narrative "script" about self-doubt that's running in your mind. The metaphors are less important than the reality that metacognition is something that your brain actually does—it's not a vague, theoretical concept; it's a neural reality. We all have this ability, and whichever metaphor you prefer to explain it is fine if it works.

REPORTER: And by "works," you mean it gets us to the life outcomes we want?

EXPLORER: Exactly, and that's the essence of pragmatic adaptation. Our brains are incredible adaptive marvels of nature, and they include "tools" like metacognition to enhance their adaptive abilities. Each day we must pragmatically adapt to the worlds (societies, cultures) we live in, and what we've discovered during the exploration is that we can harness our brains' adaptive power to enrich our lives.

REPORTER: Along the way, what are the milestones that someone should expect to reach during the exploration? Any especially noteworthy peaks?

EXPLORATION: We've found that when we figure out how to use metacognition to harness our brains' adaptive power, a few things happen—the "milestones" you're talking about. People can expect to experience three significant effects. They will become more autonoetic, more ego-symmetric, and more effective conscious self-narrators.

REPORTER: Please explain each of those.

EXPLORER: By autonoetic, I mean that they'll attain a higher degree of self-awareness. Research shows that becoming more autonoetic has several benefits, such as higher levels of creativity, heightened ability to apply learned knowledge, and more adaptability in terms of thinking through problems.

By ego-symmetric, I mean they'll attain a greater ability to detach from thoughts and feelings that conflict with the achievement of their goals—the outcomes they want in life

By conscious self-narrative, I mean they'll become the reviewers, editors, and writers of those "scripts" we mentioned. Instead of internal and external narratives directing their lives, they'll assert more conscious control of their own narratives.

REPORTER: And then what?

EXPLORER: And then they become better adaptors. And the outcomes of pragmatically adapting to our lives reinforce the process. Ever heard the phrase "Success breeds success"? Well, you could modify that and more accurately say, "Adaptation breeds success."

REPORTER: Well folks, there you have it. "Adaptation breeds success." One last question, what are you going to do next?

EXPLORER: That's the easiest question of all, and you just answered it. I am going to *do*.

KNOW

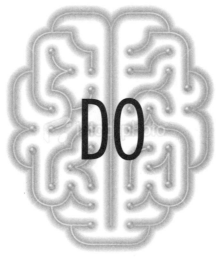

DO

EXPAND

THE THOUGHT BOX

30 TOOLS TO ENHANCE THINKING AND CATALYZE ACTION

KNOWING IS NOT ENOUGH; WE MUST APPLY. WILLING IS NOT ENOUGH; WE MUST DO.

— *Johann Wolfgang von Goethe*

THIS SECTION of the book moves us from theory to practice—from knowledge to action. To argue that 30 is an adequate number to capture the tools science has provided for improving our thinking is like arguing that understanding our solar system is an adequate means of deconstructing the mysteries of the universe. Having said that, 30 is a pretty good start, and that is precisely what I want this section to achieve—to provide a solid start for changing the way we think.

I've organized the tools in this section into four interrelated categories:

 Personal—chiefly addresses tools related to our internal worlds, our personal mindscapes.

External—deals with the points at which our internal worlds vector with our external realities; this is where, for example, awareness gained through cultural exposure occurs.

 Relational—addresses our interpersonal realities: how our thinking influences and is influenced by that of others.

 Biochemical—focuses on tools that catalyze biochemical (with special emphasis on neurochemical) changes that result in changes in how we think and act.

After each tool's description, you'll find a **Brain-Changer Principle (BCP)** that encapsulates the most important takeaways. (At least as I see them; you will probably find a few others—I'm hoping that you do.)

	Applications			
Tool	**Personal**	**External**	**Relational**	**Biochemical**
1. Use the Awareness Wedge	✓		✓	
2. Use the Golden Rule of Habit Change to Transform Your Behavior	✓			✓
3. Conduct a Bare-Knuckles Belief Audit of Your Goals	✓	✓		
4. Chew Gum	✓			✓
5. Write Your Own Obituary	✓			
6. Get Motivated, Not Overmotivated	✓	✓		

	Personal	External	Relational	Biochemical
			Applications	
Tool	**Personal**	**External**	**Relational**	**Biochemical**
7. Understand Your Emotional Experience Feedback Loop	✓	✓		
8. Sync Conscious and Unconscious Motivations by Checking the Forces that Shape Dishonesty	✓		✓	
9. Seek Mindful Integration	✓			
10. Enforce Periodic Campaigns of Silence	✓		✓	
11. Challenge Some of Your Judgmental Heuristics	✓	✓		
12. Boost Self-Control with a Burst of Glucose	✓			✓
13. Learn to Stop Thoughts	✓	✓		
14. Create an Impromptu Brain Sync	✓	✓	✓	
15. Just Keep Doing Something	✓	✓		
16. Sleep to Keep Your Cerebral Circuits from Overheating	✓			✓
17. Assert Thyself	✓		✓	

Tool	Applications			
	Personal	External	Relational	Biochemical
18. Manifest Your Resilience	✓	✓	✓	
19. Conduct a Failure Assessment	✓			
20. Keep Tabs on Your Chemical Thresholds	✓			✓
21. Make a Study of People Who Love What They Do	✓		✓	
22. Boost Your Metaphor Quotient (MQ)	✓			
23. Increase Your Culture Dosage	✓	✓		
24. Begin an Enriching Routine of Reading Challenging Literature and Watching Challenging Movies	✓	✓		
25. Think…*Really* Think…About Achievement	✓	✓	✓	
26. Understand the Elements of Self-Regulation	✓	✓		✓
27. Move Your Body to Manage Your Mind	✓			✓
28. Study the Minds of Metacognitive Pioneers	✓	✓		

	Applications			
Tool	Personal	External	Relational	Biochemical
29. Put Yourself Through a Catastrophic Loss Exercise	✓			
30. Meet the 12 Metarepresentations of Mind	✓	✓		

1. Use the Awareness Wedge

HUMAN BEINGS, BY CHANGING THE INNER ATTITUDES OF THEIR MINDS,
CAN CHANGE THE OUTER ASPECTS OF THEIR LIVES.

—*William James*

One of the most basic metacognitive tools we have at our disposal is our ability to pause before taking the next action in a sequence of actions. This ability has been described in a variety of ways in the psychological literature. *Mindhacker* authors Ron and Marty Hale-Evans use the term "semantic pause" and divide the ability by duration and depth. They use the term "tactical pause" to describe a "low-level" and immediate stop, and the term "contemplative pause" to describe a "high-level" detachment that allows for greater depth of deliberation before acting. The ability is also sometimes referred to as a "cognitive pause," which highlights the fact that we enact the ability in our conscious mind space. It's a type of antithetical thinking that causes a flashing red cognitive stop sign to keep us from taking another step.[1]

However it's described, the awareness wedge is routinely underused. Put into wider practice, it could both prevent actions that cause negative outcomes and encourage actions that promote positive outcomes. To quote the Hale-Evanses, it "forces awareness into a situation to either wake us up or calm and clarify." For example, if you find yourself in a contentious discussion with a coworker and feel the tension escalating as you both try to make your points, an immediate, tactical pause can give you the small amount of time you need to consider whether your next statement is going to contribute constructively or just add propane to the fire. The same thing could be said of an argument with a significant other; inserting an immediate awareness wedge into the discussion before you fire off the next volley of words could prevent an unnecessary emotional explosion and its inevitable fallout.

The longer-duration variety of wedge is exactly what you need to check yourself when considering your next thought-action combination in higher-order decisions, such as buying a car or a house, getting married, or taking a new job. We usually think we already do this before big decisions, because they consume so much of our mental energy, but there is a significant difference between a flood of mental energy and a directed, deliberate focusing of energy on a specific decision. Simply spending a lot of time thinking about something is no guarantee that all of our anguished processing will result in the best outcome. Using the awareness wedge instead demands that we stop the thinking flood, reconsider how we are thinking about a given situation, and redirect our mental energy. This may result, for instance, in breaking the decision into smaller parts and directing our thinking to address each part, working toward the whole. Or it could mean that we reconsider our basic motivations for pursuing an outcome that we've been taking for granted is the right one.

Using the awareness wedge for short- or long-term situations takes practice, especially if we find it difficult to question our motivations. A stout dose of humility is required to stop and reassess whether "winning" an argument is the best outcome. Also needed is a willingness to face adversity (along with fear and anxiety) by stopping and questioning our reasons for making a major decision. Doing so, however, could make all the difference in the short and long term.

Brain-Changer Principle (BCP): We have the ability to pause our thinking, for short and long durations—even under intense pressure—which provides an invaluable opportunity to reevaluate before taking the next action step; the effects of this seemingly basic ability can be profound.

2. Use the Golden Rule of Habit Change to Transform Your Behavior

SUCCESS IS THE ABILITY TO GO FROM ONE FAILURE TO ANOTHER WITH NO LOSS OF ENTHUSIASM.

—*Winston Churchill*

Habits are feedback loops that we run over and over until a behavior occurs without conscious thought. As described in Charles Duhigg's book, *The Power of Habit*, the habit feedback loop is composed of three elements: a cue, which initiates the behavior; the routine, which is the cued behavior; and the reward, which is what we're seeking from the behavior.[2]

For example, you can break down a smoking habit like this: the cue is stress; the routine is lighting up a cigarette; the reward is mental stimulation (because nicotine is actually a stimulant) that counterbalances the stress. A sugary-food habit might look like this: the cue is anxiety; the routine is eating a donut; the reward is a temporary curbing of anxiety by the blast of glucose entering your bloodstream.

The "Golden Rule of Habit Change" (described by Duhigg and well documented in years of research) is that to change a habit, you must focus on the routine, not the cue or reward. In the smoking example, you cannot eliminate stress (the cue), nor can you eliminate your desire for mental stimulation to relieve the stress (the reward). The only part of the feedback loop you can change is the routine. So instead of lighting up, a new routine of drinking coffee could provide the same reward. (This gets a little tricky when we're talking about chemical routines like smoking, because nicotine is physically and psychologically addictive, but it's important to remember that the Golden Rule may have to be implemented over and over before a new routine displaces the old; in other words, it takes as long as it takes, and for different people, that time period varies).

What about nonchemical habits, like falling onto the couch to watch hours of television after a stressful day at work? Here again, the cue is stress; the routine is hours of sedentary TV viewing; the reward is mental escape from stress. In this case we have a little more flexibility because several different routines could replace watching TV—and perhaps the new routine won't entirely displace the old, but will replace enough of it to alter the habit and yield a better outcome. For example, walking for an hour and then watching TV for an hour or two could be the new routine that replaces hours of sofa sitting.

No matter the habit, the point is that we can force the crux of the issue—the routine—into conscious mind space and change it. Start by choosing one habit you want to change and stay with it until it works. Remember, also, that for ingrained habits you're going to wrestle with unconsciously controlled behaviors for as long as it takes, and it's impossible to forecast that duration for you, me, or anyone else. Think of it this way: you are lowering a crane into the unconscious and hooking into a routine that's been running in a continuous feedback loop for a long time—probably years. Temper your expectations for how quickly you can change the routine, but don't give up hope that you can. The research is quite clear that if you stick with it, you will.

> **BCP: Understanding how habits work empowers us to alter them—not in unrealistic, wholesale ways, but in realistic, pragmatic ways that will affect genuine changes in our brains and our lives.**

3. Conduct a Bare-Knuckles Belief Audit of Your Goals

IF ONE ADVANCES CONFIDENTLY IN THE DIRECTION OF HIS DREAMS,
AND ENDEAVORS TO LIVE THE LIFE WHICH HE HAS IMAGINED, HE WILL
MEET WITH A SUCCESS UNEXPECTED IN COMMON HOURS.

—*Henry David Thoreau*

Your brain is an energy hog and energy miser at the same time.[3] It's an energy hog in that it consumes roughly 20 percent of your body's circulating blood glucose; it's a miser in that it won't allow the body to consume additional energy without a good reason. A "good reason" is defined in this case as a goal with a reasonable chance of success. For your brain to approve dispensing more energy to accomplish whatever task is in front of you, something has to "click." That something happens in our conscious mind space, and it's called *belief*.

Our cynical culture has made belief into a punch line, but our brains are not amused. In fact, no matter how much we want to belittle belief (or believers), it remains one of the most potent metacognitive tools at our disposal, and we ignore it at our peril. Here's the simple fact borne out by reams of research: until we believe that we can do something, we are not allotted the resources to do it.

In their book *Maximum Brainpower*, Shlomo Breznitz and Collins Hemingway describe the belief dynamic as working both for and against us, because both hope and despair are forms of belief. Despair is the belief that our situation cannot improve, and when we embrace this form of belief our brain responds by diverting energy away from action to improve our circumstances (because we believe it's hopeless) and into an eddy of negative rumination, fueling the downward spiral. Despair begets despair, which is why it is clinically recognized as the psychological condition most likely to lead to suicide; paradoxical as it may sound, it takes belief to end your life.[4]

Hope is the belief that our situation can and will improve no matter what, and when we fully embrace it, our brain responds with a deluge of mental energy to enable reaching the hopeful outcome. In the words of Breznitz and Hemingway, "Both hope and despair are self-fulfilling prophecies."

So ask yourself, when you review your life objectives: Just how much do you believe you can accomplish them? I call this a "bare-knuckles belief audit" because it's essential that you don't lie to yourself. Make a concerted effort to force the issue into conscious mind space and take a close look. Whether what you find is good, bad, or ugly, what matters most is that you are identifying voids in your belief commitment to every goal. In the process, you may trim down your list, deciding that some goals are simply not worthy of fully invested belief.

Remember, it's an audit—a self-enforced audit, but an audit, to be sure—and it may not be the most pleasurable way to spend your time. But you will not tap into the full array of mental resources available to you unless you hold yourself accountable for how much you genuinely believe you'll succeed. Think of your brain as an investor you're pitching to inject massive resources into your project, but the only way to make that happen is by convincing this miserly investor to fully commit. Your pitch to the investor is going to happen on the stage that is your conscious mind space, and the belief audit is how you're going to prepare yourself to make the winning pitch.

BCP: Belief is an essential brain changer; without it, your brain will not provide the resources required to accomplish whatever is in your sights.

4. Chew Gum

LITTLE THINGS MAKE BIG THINGS HAPPEN.

—*John Wooden*

Would you believe that while standing in line to pay for your groceries, you are but an arm's length away from a potent neurochemical catalyst that costs less than a single pill of any antidepressant? Yes, gum—wonderful, flavorful, get-your-jaws-moving gum—is an unlikely object of cognitive-science research that turns out to possess qualities Mr. Wrigley would never have guessed.

Gum has been studied for its beneficial effects on memory, alertness, anxiety reduction, appetite suppression, mood, and learning. Attributes of gum that have gone under the microscope include its flavor, texture, and density, to name a few.

The hunch that spawned gum studies was that chewing gum might increase blood flow to the brain, and that could in turn spark other important effects. Studies such as one out of Cardiff University in the UK take a comprehensive view of gum's potential across multiple areas: learning, mood, memory, and intelligence. The findings in this case were that both alertness and intellectual performance were increased in gum-chewing subjects while they chewed; memory showed no significant improvement.

Other studies have found that some aspects of memory seem to be improved by chewing gum, particularly immediate and delayed word recall, while others are not. An especially significant 2011 study found that chewing gum before taking a test improved performance, but chewing gum throughout the test did not. The possible reason for this result is that chewing gum may warm up the brain, something gum researchers refer to as "mastication-induced arousal." In fact, chewing gum for about twenty minutes is on a par with mild exercise in terms of sending more blood to the brain. Continuing to chew after the warm-up period seems to have required too much jaw work, and burning more energy negated the benefits.[5]

Studies have also found gum to be an effective anxiety buster, though just why is anything but clear. A 2009 study, for instance, found that under laboratory conditions chewing gum resulted in reduced cortisol levels (cortisol is frequently called the "stress hormone") and a reduction in overall anxiety.[6]

And it may also be true that prescription antidepressants have a far cheaper rival wrapped in foil just waiting to be chewed. A study conducted in Tokyo suggests that prolonged gum chewing activates a part of the brain (the ventral part of the prefrontal cortex) that in turns sets off a cascade of effects resulting in fewer feelings of depression. In fact, chewing gum seems to induce suppression of "nociceptive responses" in general—a bit of jargon loosely translated as "pain in the brain."[7]

True enough, the reasons for these effects are still a bit speculative, but the wealth of research pointing to benefits of gum chewing can't be ignored. We may not yet know why it benefits the brain, but few things are simpler, cheaper, or less risky than tossing a stick of gum in your mouth for a good chew.

> **BCP: Chewing gum is an example of a brain-changer tool that almost all of us have easy access to and can try. The research suggests that it may be the simplest thing you can do to give your brain a neurochemical boost.**

5. Write Your Own Obituary

WORDS ARE, OF COURSE, THE MOST POWERFUL DRUG USED BY MANKIND.

—*Rudyard Kipling*

While morbid at first blush, taking time to write your own obituary can be an incredibly clarifying exercise. As one form of what is often called "paradoxical therapy," it accomplishes several things at once. First, it forces you to consider yourself from a detached perspective, because you will naturally adopt the mindset of someone reading the obituary. Second, it dislodges fragments of memory and places them into conscious mind space. When crafting your obituary, you'll consciously review some of these memory fragments, which you may learn have been dormant for a long time. Third, it engenders a form of self-honesty that is difficult to otherwise achieve, because you are writing the last documented summary of who you are.

The twist is that it will also challenge your self-narrative—and that's perhaps the most important objective of all. As discussed in the first part of this book, self-narrative is the thread that holds the elements of our personalities together; it's the reason you are an "I" and not a "we." Our brain has developed this ability for good reason; namely, we aren't able to hold in consciousness all of the contradictory aspects of the self without psychologically fragmenting and losing a necessary sense of control. When you write your obituary, the narrative you've been living will look back at you, and you will consciously engage questions about who you have been, who you are, and who you want to be.

Finally, writing your obituary will put you in touch with the proctor of your final exam—the test none of us can avoid taking. While dwelling on death isn't beneficial, coming to terms with mortality is a grounding experience that places the events of one's life in perspective. What appears to be overwhelming now may not seem so important when you're reviewing your life, and maybe other aspects of your present reality will rise to the surface as more compelling and worth more of your attention.

Start by giving yourself a word-count goal—say, 500 words. Then begin constructing yourself with those words, focusing on what you want others to know about you. But unlike a promotional writer, you aren't engaging this exercise to methodically retouch your blemishes. Tell your story the way you want to tell it, but consider the totality of *you*. If you were married four times, that's part of your story. If you served time in prison, that's part of your story. Just remember that these realities, like the ones that speak well of you, need context, and that's what you're giving them in your 500-word exposition. Write as many versions of your obituary as you like until you have in hand a written self-narrative that you believe tells an unvarnished short story of who you are. Then put it aside and revisit it every few months as a work in progress, each time changing it in some way to account for your ongoing narrative. You'll be surprised at what changes along the way—more precisely, at how your self-perspective changes.

BCP: Writing your own obituary is not much fun to begin with, but when you've written it, you will immediately realize that it has significantly and constructively changed your perspective from that moment forward.

6. Get Motivated, Not Overmotivated

HE DID EACH SINGLE THING, AS IF HE DID NOTHING ELSE.

—*Charles Dickens*

Believe it or not, it's possible to become overmotivated to achieve a goal. Motivation is a prerequisite for success in most cases, but there's a limit to how much it helps before it starts working against you. This was craftily illustrated in a study called "Choking on the Money," which offered participants cash for doing well on the iconic video game Pac-Man. Researchers varied the amounts of cash to elicit varying levels of motivation among the players, with the hypothesis that the greater the cash reward, the greater the motivation to succeed— and, paradoxically, the greater the cost of failure.[8]

While they played the game, the research team analyzed participants' brains with an fMRI (functional magnetic resonance imaging) machine. What they found was that players with the most cash on the line had the highest level of activity in their brains' reward centers (the combination of brain areas associated with pursuit of rewards, be they material, like money, or otherwise). These players also made the most mistakes. What was happening in the high-stakes players' brains to cause this odd effect?

As it turns out, the allure of more cash flooded the players' reward centers with too much dopamine—the reward neurotransmitter— for their own good. As Chris Berdik explains in his book *Mind Over Mind*, dopamine signals what University of Michigan biopsychologist Kent Berridge dubbed "incentive salience," which is what transforms mere predictions of a reward into the motivation to obtain it. All of us need dopamine to change "want" to "pursuit" in order to achieve anything, but our brains' reward centers can be overwhelmed with "want" to the point that a deluge of dopamine handicaps our capacity to consciously evaluate and control the pursuit. That's what happened in the brains of the Pac-Man players with the most money on the line. They made the most mistakes of all the participants (and lost the most money—the exact opposite of what they wanted). To quote Berdik, "Motivated people succeed. Overmotivated people fail."[9]

The solution is not an easy one, but research suggests that we are equipped with the ability to tune down the reward center before dopamine floods its circuits and makes controlling the outcome increasingly difficult. This is a consciousness challenge, because the motivations for pursuit of any given reward are not entirely known to us; to an extent they remain unconscious. If it sounds odd to hear that we are not totally, consciously aware of why we are pursuing a goal, welcome to the strange arena of the brain where not everything is as it seems. The good news is that we can obtain a degree of conscious control over goal pursuit by thinking through the elements of the reward feedback loop. Much like understanding how the engine of a car can become flooded with fuel, when we understand the working parts of the reward feedback loop, we increase our chances of preventing overmotivation. The most critical part is the perceived, expected benefit of reaching the goal (reward). In many cases, the expectation is not in proportion to the actual benefit—though the "actual" benefit may be unclear at first glance. How do we know if our expectation of the reward is in the proverbial ballpark of the actual reward? We can't know for sure—but the very act of consciously tempering expectations will slow the loop's velocity. If we end up being dead-on correct about the benefits of the reward, all the better.

BCP: Motivation is essential, but overmotivation is self-defeating. Understand the perception threshold between the two and avoid crossing it to get the most out of your brain's capacity for achievement. Just because a little

medicine is useful doesn't mean twice the amount will produce twice the results; the opposite (or worse) is almost always true.

7. Understand Your Emotional Experience Feedback Loop

ALL EMOTIONS ARE PURE WHICH GATHER YOU AND LIFT YOU UP; THAT EMOTION IS IMPURE WHICH SEIZES ONLY ONE SIDE OF YOUR BEING AND SO DISTORTS YOU.

—*Rainer Maria Rilke*

Your emotional experience can be traced using a feedback loop analysis as we have for several other dynamics discussed throughout this book. However, emotional experience is a significantly complex feedback loop.

The first element is background feeling—the emotional setting, if you will, for all emotional experiences. Psychologists David Watson and Lee Anna Clark describe this as *stream of affect*.[10] A stream of affect may be positive, negative, or neutral, and it may be noticeable or unnoticed. You may wake up one day and feel "off" emotionally (the classic "wrong side of the bed" feeling), but not be able to pinpoint exactly why. Or, you may find yourself especially positive and open to new experiences, again without a specific cause. These are both examples of the stream of affect that sets our daily emotional background.

Stream of affect leads to the next level of emotional intensity: *mood state*. Moods are felt more acutely than stream of affect states, and they may last for hours, days, weeks, or longer. Someone's mood is typically what "rubs off" most on those around him or her. If you are anxious over time, others read your mood and may steer clear of you for a while because you're making them anxious (via another well-studied psychological phenomenon, the "emotional contagion" effect). Or, if you're consistently positive, others may be drawn to you because your confidence feeds their fire.

Mood state leads to the most intense level of emotional experience—the onset of an *emotion*. Emotion is not synonymous with "emotional experience," but is rather a specific, usually short-term event that manifests in response to a trigger. Triggers can be external to the self or internal (such as deeply felt trauma relived through memory). Externally, emotions give rise to a panoply of facial and bodily gestures, and internally to subjective feelings that set the stage for "action tendencies."

Action tendencies include specific responses like aggression, despair, defensiveness, exhilaration, affection, forgiveness, or fear. The intensity of the emotion dictates how much of your attention is dedicated to it, and when it's felt intensely enough you may be controlled by it. As Dr. Shelley Carson describes in her book *Your Creative Brain*, complete control by an emotion is called "emotional hijacking." Examples include rage, panic, and extreme despair—which in turn can lead to violence, nervous breakdown, and suicide. At this point, the action tendency has become an "action imperative," and when that transition is made, we have little control over our emotionally driven actions.[11]

By understanding these points in the emotional experience feedback loop, we can engage conscious control well before reaching the action-imperative stage. For example, during the onset of a mood state, we can insert a pause and self-reflect on why we're feeling down, up, or otherwise. We may discover at this stage that we're ripe for a negative trigger to send us into dangerous emotional territory, or, conversely, that we're feeling so confident that raising a red flag isn't warranted. The important thing is not to avoid the experience of intensely felt emotion, but to try our best to honestly forecast where our emotional state is going.

This isn't easy to do, and the psychological literature is full of examples of emotional forecasting gone awry—but our inability to perfectly predict what's coming next isn't reason to avoid trying our best to make the most accurate prediction possible. If at the mood-state stage we can redirect our thoughts, and thus help redirect our emotional trajectory, we can prevent unrealistically negative or positive action imperatives from taking hold. This redirection is fed back into the loop and changes our emotional experience in this and future experiences. With time and practice, we gain greater control of our emotional experience—not draining it of its intensity, but directing it as best as possible to achieve improved outcomes.

> **BCP: Emotional experience isn't one process—it's a continuum of feedback processes. Knowing how one process leads to the next enables us to adapt our thinking at the right time to alter the outcome.**

8. Sync Conscious and Unconscious Motivations by Checking the Forces that Shape Dishonesty

TO DOUBT EVERYTHING OR TO BELIEVE EVERYTHING ARE TWO EQUALLY CONVENIENT SOLUTIONS; BOTH DISPENSE WITH THE NECESSITY OF REFLECTION.

—*Jules Henri Poincaré*

Syncing conscious and unconscious motivations is a significant part of asserting metacognitive control to improve outcomes, and there are several ways of accomplishing this. One is offered by psychologist and behavioral economist Dan Ariely in his book *The (Honest) Truth About Dishonesty*. Ariely focuses on the "dark side of creativity" to throw light on a tendency of the creative brain that makes it easier for us to reinterpret information in self-serving ways. The irony is that this same ability allows us to envision novel solutions to tough problems and find "original paths" to reach our goals.[12]

To quote Ariely, "Putting our creative minds to work can help us have our cake and eat it too, and create stories in which we're always the hero, never the villain." The difficulty is that on one hand we have in mind positive, desired outcomes, but on the other we're influenced by the dark side of creativity, which puts us in, to use Ariely's words, a "tight spot." To help us navigate out of this spot, he offers a summary of the forces that shape dishonesty. His research indicates that eight main forces drive dishonesty, both within ourselves and outwardly:

1. Ability to rationalize
2. Conflicts of interest
3. Creativity
4. One immoral act
5. Being depleted
6. Others benefiting from our dishonesty
7. Watching others behave dishonestly
8. Cultures that provide examples of dishonesty

He also offers four factors that decrease dishonesty:

1. Pledges
2. Signatures
3. Moral reminders
4. Supervision

Finally, he says that two factors appear to have no discernible effect on dishonesty:

1. Amount of money to be gained (surprisingly)
2. Probability of being caught

The metacognitive tool in this case isn't to jettison creativity to avoid its "dark side," but rather to keep a mental tally of the factors Ariely's research suggests will predispose us to acting dishonestly. Consider his work a flashlight that illuminates one of the many bridges between our unconscious and conscious motivations. We may, for example, not consciously realize that feeling depleted—low on energy and other physical resources—is unconsciously predisposing us to dishonesty. If we know this, then we can look to Ariely's list of factors that decrease dishonesty, and perhaps seek ways to insert moral reminders into our daily lives as a counterbalance against dishonesty. A moral reminder can be an actual, physical reminder in your daily planner, or a mental note that you refer to often.

The most salient point Ariely makes is that we lie to ourselves as much as or more than we lie to others. His work is of critical importance to knowing how to identify self-deception before we are swept up in it. This is hard medicine and a difficult tool to implement, but it's less difficult than reaping the whirlwind of the patterns of dishonesty that form when we're not conscious of the underlying factors that predispose us to thinking and acting dishonestly.

> **BCP: Part of asserting metacognitive control involves pulling the veil off of our unconscious motivations. This isn't easy to do, but using a deception-detection tool can help shed light on self-serving motivations we're prone to ignore.**

9. Seek Mindful Integration

BE REALLY WHOLE, AND ALL THINGS WILL COME TO YOU.

—Lao Tzu

Psychologist and author Daniel Siegel has made an enormous contribution to understanding the human mind by elucidating what he describes as "mindful integration"—the integration of the mind's flow of both energy and information.[13]

Energy is the capacity to carry out an action—whether it's something basic like moving your arm, or a more complex action like thinking a thought. Information is anything that symbolizes something other than itself. For example, a stone itself is not information, but the word "stone" is information. Our minds must identify and analyze the letters (symbols) in the word "stone" to equate it with the physical object.

To quote Siegel, "Knowing that our minds regulate the flow of both energy and information allows us to feel the reality of these two forms of mental experience and act on them instead of getting lost in them."

Siegel contends that integration occurs when we understand that this regulation of energy and information isn't only occurring within our brains and nervous systems, but also between our mind and others' minds. In other words, integration is *relational*.

Put another way, your mind isn't only what your brain is doing—it's what your brain is doing within the social and cultural context in which you live. Mind is a relational, not an individual concept. Understanding this allows us to see more clearly why we are influenced and affected by the thoughts of others, and why and how we influence others. The relational dynamic of mind isn't contained within your skull, and the flow of energy and information is interactional.

BCP: No one is an island, and no mind is just a brain. Remember the role others play in the ongoing emergence of your mind.

10. Enforce Periodic Campaigns of Silence

IT IS SWEET TO LET THE MIND UNBEND ON OCCASION.

—*Horace, Roman Poet*

Our brain's command center, the prefrontal cortex, has evolved to listen because information often comes in the form of sound—but not only external sound. The noise generated from within our brains can also be enough to stymie concentration.

In their book *Words Can Change Your Brain*, Andrew Newberg and Mark Robert Waldman recommend cultivating inner silence so that we can learn to give our fullest attention to what other people say. "Unconsciously they will know when we're distracted by our inner speech, and the lack of interest they perceive will make them distance themselves from you."[14]

The metacognitive tool here is twofold: learning to shut out external noise and internal noise. Of the two, external noise is the easier to handle because you can use any number of tools to create a virtual sound isolation booth, including the use of sound itself. By looping certain songs using headphones, you can encourage your brain to enter a theta-beta brainwave state—the state most conducive to calm contemplation.[15] This is largely trial and error, because you'll have to discover what works best for you. I've found that the best songs are those that either don't have lyrics or have lyrics I'm so familiar with that they don't require additional mental energy to decipher. They "roll" over my mind in calming waves. I've found this technique especially useful in coffee shops. I enjoy the social environment of the shops but find the random cacophony of noises too distracting to work, so I loop certain songs with my smartphone and headphones and create a virtual sound booth in the midst of the otherwise active social atmosphere.

To cultivate inner silence, you can try a variety of techniques including mindfulness meditation (also described in some detail by Newberg and Walden). But in my experience, there's a symbiotic relationship between blocking out random, external sound and the cultivation of inner silence. "Silence" in this case doesn't mean "absence of sound," but rather a steadiness of mentally undemanding sound. Experiment with different techniques until you find a few that work best for you and then enforce periods of "silence" that will ultimately sharpen your focus and attention.

> **BCP: Periodic external and internal silence is essential for enhancing focus and improving our ability to truly listen. Sometimes you must get out of the chaotic flow of external and internal noise, or else be swept away by it.**

11. Challenge Some of Your Judgmental Heuristics

YOU ARE TODAY WHERE YOUR THOUGHTS HAVE BROUGHT YOU; YOU
WILL BE TOMORROW WHERE YOUR THOUGHTS TAKE YOU.

—James Allen

One of the most useful dynamics of our unconscious minds is some-thing cognitive scientists call "automaticity." In brief, automaticity is the shortcut our brains use to accomplish things that would oth-erwise require lengthy, deliberate thought. In these cases, acting automatically—our brain determines—is in our best interest, while acting deliberately might get us killed.

One of the classic examples of this dynamic is the "snake in the road." Let's say you're walking down a quiet mountain path and a few yards in front of you is what appears to be a coiled snake. Automati-cally, without the least conscious deliberation, you jump back. In fact, you jump back before you confirm that this thing on the path really is a snake. After a few seconds, you notice that the object isn't moving at all, so you slowly and cautiously approach it. Only then do you realize that it isn't a snake, but a thick, dark, twisted stick.

The shortcut your brain used to make your body jump back is an evolved, hardwired judgmental heuristic—a mental rule—that is there to help ensure your survival (or at least increase your chances of survival). Using this shortcut, your brain prevents you from getting too close too quickly and conducting a potentially fatal inspection of the ominous object in your path.

The good news about this judgmental heuristic is self-evident: it can save your life. The bad news is that it can be, and frequently is, hijacked by cultural forces—some of them perniciously unscrupulous. Snake-oil salesmen have exploited this for years. If you encounter a product that claims to improve health by bolstering the immune sys-tem against any oncoming viral or bacterial threats, your first reaction might be to buy it. Who doesn't want that sort of health boost? It's a "no-brainer" to buy it. Thinking it through, of course, reveals that you should just walk on by and save your money: the claim is patently false. No such product exists. Viruses and bacteria have thrived on this planet far longer than we have, and will continue to long after we're gone. We don't even have a cure for the common cold! The product's claim leverages our unthinking desire for better health, which in turns fuels an impulse to open our wallets.

> **BCP: Judgmental heuristics are essential to our survival, but can also predispose us to faulty decision making. Knowing when a judgmental heuristic is being exploited educates our thinking and improves future outcomes.**

12. Boost Self-Control with a Burst of Glucose

MY FAULT, MY FAILURE, IS NOT IN THE PASSIONS I HAVE, BUT IN MY LACK OF CONTROL OF THEM.

—*Allen Ginsberg*

If you're struggling to keep your self-control on track, keep a bottle of lemonade made with real sugar handy. You won't have to drink it, just swish and gargle when you're feeling like giving up.

That's the finding of research published in the journal *Psychological Science*.[16] Researchers from the University of Georgia recruited 51 students who performed two tasks to test self-control. The first task, which previous research has shown to deplete self-control, was tediously crossing out all the Es on a page from a statistics book. Then, participants performed what is known as the Stroop task. They were asked to identify the color of various words flashed on a screen, which spell out the names of other colors. The Stroop task's goal is to turn off the student's tendency to read the words (which is easy to do) and instead see the colors (which is harder to do).

Half of the students rinsed their mouths with lemonade sweetened with sugar while performing the Stroop task, the other half with Splenda-sweetened lemonade. Students who rinsed with sugar, rather than artificial sweetener, were significantly faster at responding to the color rather than the word.

Why? It seems that the glucose in the lemonade triggers the brain's motivational centers simply by touching the tongue, giving the participants the extra push to complete the harder task.

"Researchers used to think you had to drink the glucose and get it into your body to give you the energy to [have] self control," said UGA psychology professor Leonard Martin, co-author of the study. "After this trial, it seems that glucose stimulates the simple carbohydrate sensors on the tongue. This, in turn, signals the motivational centers of the brain where our self-related goals are represented. These signals tell your body to pay attention."

Since glucose is the brain's primary energy source, it makes sense that a quick shot of sugar would crank up attention. But according to the researchers, this study suggests that the sugar is providing more than a simple energy boost.

"It doesn't just crank up your energy, but it cranks up your personal investment in what you are doing. Clicking into the things that are important to you makes those self-related goals salient," said Martin.

The theory behind Martin's statement is called "emotive enhancement," in which something (in this case sugar) leads a person to pay attention to their goals and not automatically act on an urge to stop investing self-control when they're feeling depleted. An example might be staying an extra half an hour at the gym when you're feeling like calling it quits.

"The glucose seems to be good at getting you to stop an automatic response such as reading the words in the Stroop task and to substitute the second, harder one in its place, such as saying the color the word is printed in," he said. "It can enhance emotive investment and self-relevant goals."

BCP: Like chewing gum, this is a simple tool that most of us can try. Research suggests that a shot of glucose is often

exactly what your brain needs to get an edge—just a swish now and then can produce real change.

13. Learn to Stop Thoughts

WE CAN'T SOLVE PROBLEMS BY USING THE SAME KIND OF THINKING WE USED WHEN WE CREATED THEM.

—*Albert Einstein*

The ability to manage conscious thought is indispensable in the metacognitive toolbox. It's the core discipline that makes metacognition such a powerful internal asset. Two techniques are especially crucial: thought stopping and thought postponement.

Thought stopping is a behavioral tool used in clinical psychology to help patients control anxiety, anger, and chronic fear. While there are various ways to implement this technique, I'm endorsing one described in Shelley Carson's book *Your Creative Brain*, which requires you to have a few three-by-five index cards and a pen handy.[17] Using the technique, you will simply tell yourself to stop particular thoughts as soon as you notice them, using either verbal commands or mental images. The commands could include:

"Don't go there."

"Mentally walk away."

"These thoughts won't help the situation."

Mental images could include a stop sign or a hand raised in a "Stop!" position.

Carson recommends saying these commands to yourself when you're having thoughts you don't like, and writing them down on an index card. She recommends writing a total of six commands (or images), four on one side of the card and two on the other. Keep the card with you and use it whenever you have to. With time, the commands and images will become automatic responses to negative thoughts—but you have to give the technique time to work. At first it could take several minutes each time you use a command or image; the time will eventually diminish as you gain greater control.

Dr. Daniel Amen, in his book *Change Your Brain, Change Your Life*, discusses research on the cingulate system of the brain, which allows us to shift attention from one thing to another—whether tangible or intangible.[18] When this system is impaired in even a minor way, we have a tendency to get locked into negative thoughts and to have difficulty seeing the options in situations. Our minds enter a dysfunctional thought loop that feels impossible to exit.

The first step to overcoming cingulate system dysfunction, according to Amen, is to notice when you're stuck and distract yourself. You have to make yourself aware that you're in the loop. "Whenever you find your thoughts cycling (going over and over), distract yourself from them. Get up and do something else."

BCP: Learning to stop thoughts is extremely difficult— but research shows that with time and perseverance, this cognitive tool *will* markedly change your brain. Just give it time and don't back off—this tool captures the essence of adaptation.

14. Create an Impromptu Brain Sync

LIFE SHRINKS OR EXPANDS ACCORDING TO ONE'S COURAGE.

—*Anaïs Nin*

Maybe you have experienced a similar situation: you're driving down the street and notice someone having a really difficult time parallel parking. They've managed to wedge halfway into the spot with the other half of their car jutting out dangerously into the path of traffic. The instant you see this, you can feel what the driver is feeling because you've been there. Nothing sucks quite the way getting caught in a screwed-up parallel parking situation sucks.

So now you have a decision to make. You can either drive by and let the person keep struggling, or you can try to help. You decide to try to help. You pull your car up to create a barrier between his car and oncoming traffic—a makeshift shelter that allows the driver to pull out of the spot and rearrange his position. Of course, he doesn't realize you are trying to help. In fact, it's likely he thinks you're pulling up to hassle him about blocking traffic, so it's important that you clarify your intentions. You wait for any cars to pass and then open your door so you can stand and motion to the driver that you're trying to help. The driver opens his window and waves, signaling that your message has been received. Now you're in this together.

Inevitably, people begin honking, yelling, and making certain gestures at you and the driver. It doesn't matter. By making a decision to help and then following up that decision with action, you've synced your believing brain with that of the driver. You believe that offering assistance, even at some risk to yourself, to help this person succeed is worthwhile, and your belief is bridging the gap between the two of you. Would the driver have eventually parked successfully without your help? Maybe, maybe not—but that isn't the point. The point, illustrated in this innocuous example, is that whenever you align your thoughts and actions with a belief that helping someone else is worthwhile, you've initiated an impromptu brain sync with that person's brain—and by doing so you've infused his or her brain with a sense of belief that success is attainable.

The phrase "pay it forward" actually has a strong neurobiological underpinning. When we witness positive action to help someone succeed, our brain registers the event as evidence of our capability to do the same. In other words, helping someone succeed becomes an attainable "reward" (in cognitive-science parlance), and we actually start looking for opportunities to attain it. This is excellent brain medicine because it builds neural connections around altruistic belief; in a very real sense, our brains grow from the experience.

The tool here is deceptively simple: the next time you have an opportunity to create an impromptu brain sync with someone, take it. You'll be helping yourself as you help them.

BCP: As uncomfortable as stepping up to help someone can be, it's worth doing for more reasons than we initially realize, not the least of which is the cognitive boost we receive in the process.

15. Just Keep Doing Something

IT IS NOT BECAUSE THINGS ARE DIFFICULT THAT WE DO NOT DARE; IT IS BECAUSE WE DO NOT DARE THAT THEY ARE DIFFICULT.

— *Lucius Annaeus Seneca*

Feeling overwhelmed is a defensive response of your brain's internal threat-alarm system. When you perceive too many things happening at once, or too many pieces of a project to reasonably handle, stress hormones are triggered and your brain puts your nervous system on alert that life is far from OK. The frequent outcome of this biochemical relay is mental paralysis. "Too much" is translated as "too risky" and "too dangerous," and you experience a system-wide stoppage. The iconic Russian psychologist Ivan Pavlov (you've heard of his salivating pooches) described this tendency as "Transmarginal Inhibition"—the point at which our nervous system virtually shuts down in the face of what he called "hyper arousal."

The tool to remedy this situation is the obverse of our mental inclination. While we want to find any distraction to unplug ourselves from the surge of overwhelming energy, a more constructive policy is to alter our perspective on the problem and look for new options for tackling it. The best option may be the least obvious: restart, anywhere. Just to be clear, this isn't an appeal to the dubious virtue of randomness; it's a solid strategic change in thinking to undercut mental paralysis.

Strategic thinking discipline is another way to describe this tool. Strategy is chiefly composed of two options: (1) that which we choose to do, and (2) that which we choose *not* to do. The twist is that you can do both at the same time: choose to stop dwelling in the place where the confluence of overwhelming factors is limiting you, and choose to restart somewhere else. It doesn't matter where—just some less-fraught place where you can train your focus and make progress. That progress will yield accomplishment—however small—that will in turn spawn more progress. Work this discipline consistently and in short order you'll find yourself back on track to accomplishing your larger goal—the very same goal that not long ago was pushing you into the sand like a rogue wave. Using strategic discipline, you find a way out from under that wave and relearn your ability to ride atop it. The ability was always there—you didn't just create it while applying this tool—but you had to enact a certain discipline to make it work for you when you needed it most.

> **BCP: Strategy is choice, and by enacting strategic discipline, you can "de-paralyze" from a confluence of overwhelming factors and reposition yourself at a different part of the problem with renewed focus. The most important thing is to keep doing something and not allow the feeling of being overwhelmed to stop your progress. When you do, you allow the feeling to become a debilitating reality. Use your brain's adaptive power to change perspective and refocus to keep your energy flowing in the direction of your goals.**

16. Sleep to Keep Your Cerebral Circuits from Overheating

I WAKE TO SLEEP, AND TAKE MY WAKING SLOW.

—*Theodore Roethke*

We intuitively know that sleep is important, and a great deal of research on the health effects of sleeplessness backs up this belief. But what exactly is going on in our brains when we don't get enough shut-eye? Researchers tackled this question in a study that suggests our brains become bundles of hyperreactive nerve cells as the sleepless hours tick by. In a sense, our noggins overheat when we deprive them of necessary downtime.

The research team, led by Marcello Massimini of the University of Milan, delivered a strong magnetic current to participants' brains that set off a cascade of electrical responses throughout their nerve cells. Using nodes attached to participants' scalps, the team then measured the strength of this electrical response in the frontal cortex, a brain region that's involved in making executive decisions. This procedure was completed a day before a night of sleep deprivation and repeated afterward.

The results: participants' electrical responses were significantly stronger (in this sense, "stronger" means more chaotic and uncontained) after a night of sleep deprivation than they were the previous day. The effect was corrected by one good night's sleep.

If you're having trouble sleeping, here are a few of the most common reasons why, according to sleep research, along with ways to correct them.[19]

Sleep Inhibitors

1. Room isn't dark enough.
Ideally, your bedroom shouldn't have any lights on, especially light emitted from a TV or any electronic device. When your eyes are exposed to light during the night, your brain is tricked into thinking it's time to wake up and reduces the production of melatonin, a hormone released by your pineal gland that causes sleepiness and lowers body temperature. Light emitted by electronic devices is especially troublesome because it mimics sunlight.

2. Exercising too late.
If you exercise within three hours of trying to sleep, you'll overstimulate your metabolism and raise your heart rate, causing restlessness

and frequent awakenings throughout the night. Try to exercise in the morning, or no later than mid- to late afternoon, to get sounder sleep.

3. Drinking alcohol too late.
We tend to think of alcohol as a sleep inducer, but it actually interferes with REM sleep, causing you to feel more tired the next morning. Granted, you may feel sleepy after you drink it, but that's a short-term effect.

4. Room temperature too warm.
Your body and brain want to cool down when you sleep, but if your room is too warm you'll thwart the cool-down process. Having a fan in your room is a good idea because it will keep you cool and produce a consistent level of white noise that will help you fall asleep. Just don't get too cold, because that will disrupt sleep as well.

5. Caffeine still in your system.
The average half-life of caffeine is 5 hours, which means that you still have three-quarters of the first dose of caffeine rolling around in your system 10 hours after you drink it. Most of us drink more than one cup of coffee, and many of us drink it late in the day. If you're going to drink coffee, drink it early.

6. Clock-watching.
Though it's hard not to do, don't look at your clock when you wake up during the night. In fact, it's best to turn it around so it's not facing you. When you habitually clock-watch, you're training your circadian rhythms the wrong way, and before long you'll find yourself waking up at exactly 3:15 every night.

7. Getting up to watch TV until you're sleepy.
This is a bad idea for a few reasons. First, watching TV stimulates brain activity, which is the exact opposite of what you want to happen if your goal is to sleep soundly. Second, the light emitted from the TV is telling your brain to wake up (see #1 above).

8. Trying to problem solve in the middle of the night.
All of us wake up at times during the night, and the first thing that pops into our heads is a big problem we're worried about. The best thing you can do is stop yourself from going there and redirect your thoughts to something less stressful. If you get stuck on the worry treadmill, you'll stay awake much longer.

9. Eating protein too close to bedtime.
Protein requires a lot of energy to digest, and that keeps your digestive system churning away while you're trying to sleep—bad combination. Better to have a light carbohydrate snack.

10. Smoking before bedtime.
Smokers equate smoking with relaxing, but that's a neurochemical trick. In truth, nicotine is a stimulant. When you smoke before trying to sleep, you can expect to wake up several times throughout the night; much as you would if you drank a cup of coffee.

> **BCP: Sleep is essential to a well-functioning brain, and if you are sleep-deprived, your thinking will most assuredly suffer. Follow the suggestions provided, and make sure you're getting at least six hours of sleep a night.**

17. Assert Thyself

TO KNOW ONESELF, ONE SHOULD ASSERT ONESELF.

—Albert Camus

A brain in balance—one that isn't bounding from one extreme to the next—exhibits a certain array of traits externally. One of these is assertiveness. Like many other brain-changer tools, assertiveness is a skill that must be learned. While it may come more naturally to some than others, it is less of a natural inclination than two other commonly expressed tendencies: aggression and passivity.

In their book, *Managing Your Mind*, psychologists Gillian Butler and Tony Hope describe assertiveness skills as providing three important kinds of balance:[20]

1. The balance between aggression and passivity
2. The balance between yourself and others
3. The balance between reflecting and reacting

The word "balance" is key, because in each of the three cases noted above, assertiveness does not entirely displace one or the other position—it blends them proportionally to the situation. For example, assertiveness is not about reflecting *instead* of reacting—it strikes a balance such that one's reaction isn't untethered from reflection. It isn't about acting solely on your behalf at the expense of others—it strikes a balance between your right to have feelings and opinions and the parallel rights of others.

The problem with extreme positions that lack balance is that they encourage only one type of behavior and one type of solution to problems. To quote Butler and Hope, "Both tyrants and doormats are dominated by control: they either need to be in control or to be controlled." Extremes are the product of rigid thinking, and through their enactment in our behavior, they also enforce rigidity.

Assertiveness, on the other hand, yields flexibility. "Assertiveness opens more possible paths and leads to a more satisfactory kind of adaptation," say Gillian and Hope. With an assertive mindset, you are aware that your needs, wants, and feelings are neither more nor less important than those of other people—they are equally important.

Gillian and Hope offer a useful list of "Assertive Rights" for reference:

I have the right

- To say "I don't know"
- To say "no"

- To have an opinion and express it
- To have feelings and to express them
- To make my own decisions and deal with the consequences
- To change my mind
- To choose how to spend my time
- To make mistakes

In total, this list of Assertive Rights expresses the freedom to be yourself, and is also a reminder that the same freedom belongs to others.

> **BCP: Rigidity in thinking prevents adaptation; flexibility promotes it. To get the most from our brains' ability to adapt, we have to strike balancing acts—such as assertiveness—by learning the skills necessary to avoid extremes in both thinking and behavior.**

18. Manifest Your Resilience

IT IS IN THE KNOWLEDGE OF THE GENUINE CONDITIONS OF OUR LIFE THAT WE MUST DRAW OUR STRENGTH TO LIVE AND OUR REASON FOR ACTING.

—Simone De Beauvoir

In his book *The UltraMind Solution*, Dr. Mark Hyman provides an excellent description of one of the most essential brain-changer tools in our arsenal, resiliency: "Resiliency is that hard-to-measure quality of adapting to change, shifting with changing tides rather than drowning, seeing the glass half full, or knowing how to turn lemons into lemonade."[21]

Hyman uses the term "plasticity" synonymously with resiliency because, as he points out, the nature of the brain mirrors the nature of our thoughts, beliefs, and attitudes. "A stiff, rigid, 'hard' person-ality is reflected in stiff cells, hard, rigid plaques in the brain, and a general loss of resiliency and the ability to renew, remember, and repair."

Hyman's research leads us to a few conclusions about the power of resiliency, and why it's among the most important tools in this section. First, adaptation itself is an ongoing form of resiliency. To say that we "pragmatically adapt" to the ebbs and flows of existence means, in part, that we do not allow ourselves to be psycho-emotionally over-taken by any challenge—past, present, or future.

Here we can add a complementary term: tenacity. Resiliency requires tenacity—the drive to push through, overcome, and step above *anything* that threatens to stop us. This isn't a slogan for an athletic shoe; this is an evolutionary reality that affects everyone to varying degrees. And if your sights are set on achieving goals, it most assuredly affects you.

In consumerist cultures, resiliency loses much of its flavor because it is central to marketing campaigns spinning ultra-positive, ultra-individualist messages. Our brains adapt to these messages, and we've learned that in large part they are meaningless. We do not become more resilient or tenacious or focused by wearing the most success-fully marketed brand of athletic shoes or tight-fitting gym shirts, or anything else of the sort.

We do become more resilient by realizing the adaptive advan-tages of resiliency and acting accordingly. Knowing that our brains respond well to flexible thinking and poorly to rigid thinking, for example, empowers us to work toward greater flexibility in our thinking. That, in turns, shows us the "proof of concept" (to borrow an engineering phrase) in the positive outcomes we begin experi-encing in our lives.

BCP: Remember: flexibility promotes adaptive brain change. Resilience is all about flexibility, and you can't harness your brain's adaptive power without it.

19. Conduct a Failure Assessment

LIFE IS 440 HORSEPOWER IN A 2-CYLINDER ENGINE.

—Henry Miller

In this tool, I'm going to offer you 10 reasons why people often fail, and I want you to think about each of them and decide which ones apply to you. This assessment will open doors to changing your thinking, so don't get wrapped around the gears of the problems; instead, think through how to adjust your thinking to address them.[22]

1. You lack the all-essential component of belief.
The human brain is a powerful problem-solving and prediction-making machine, and as we've discussed, it operates via a multitude of feedback loops. Input is what matters most in the feedback-loop dynamic. What goes into the loop begins the analysis-evaluation-action process, which ultimately results in an outcome. Here's the kicker: if your input shuttle for achieving a goal lacks the critical, emotionally relevant component of belief, then the feedback loop is drained of octane from the start. Another way to say that is—why would you expect a convincingly successful outcome when you haven't convinced yourself that it's possible?

2. Other people have convinced you of your "station."
I've always thought that "know your station in life" is among the most pernicious ideas we humans have ever come up with. The only version of it I like is Tennessee Williams's: "A high station in life is earned by the gallantry with which appalling experiences are survived with grace." Love that Tennessee Williams. What's more pernicious than the idea itself is that it's often foisted upon us by other people, and they convince us that we are what we are and we'd better just live with it because, well, that's what we'll always be. Really? Says who? Show me the chapter on predetermined stations in the cosmic rule book,

please. This also gets back to the feedback loop dynamic, because if this external "station" scripting is part of your input, you can expect sub-par outcomes all the time.

3. You don't want to be a disrupter.

The word "disrupter" has taken on a mixed bag of meanings in the last few years. Reading both popular psychology and business books, I'm not sure if it's a good or a bad thing to be. One thing seems certain: the notion of disrupting anything—of being the water that breaks the rock—is scary to most of us. Disruption is perceived as a threat by our threat-sensitive brains. Disruption means that consistency, stability, and certainty might get jettisoned for a time, and that puts our hard-wired internal defense system on high alert. Sometimes, though, you have to override the alarms and move ahead anyway. If you never do, you'll never know what could happen.

4. You think, "What if I die tomorrow?"

We all think this from time to time. And sure, any of us might die tomorrow—all the more reason not to waste time thinking about it and hamstringing yourself from going after what you want to achieve. Would you rather die as a monument to mediocrity or as someone who never quit striving? Which leads to the next one...

5. You wonder how you will be remembered.

The rub here is simply, if you die tomorrow, will people remember you as someone who clung to stability like an existential life preserver? And is that what you really want? I know for a fact that many people do want exactly that, because it's a comfortable niche to occupy on the obituary page. "She/he was a good person, good friend, good..." Good is fine, but it ain't *great*. You can't strive for great achievements by dropping anchor in Goodville. My take on this is it's OK to wonder how you'll be remembered, but don't let thoughts of "good and nice and stable" affect that all-important feedback loop. If you do, your brain will be happy to oblige with lots of good and little else.

6. You think there must be a preestablished role for your life, and you might be screwing with it.

This one also touches on the "station" idea discussed above, but it goes deeper than that. We are prone to believing in something psychologists call "agency." We want to believe there's a reason for everything, and that everything has a prime mover—an agent, whether human or otherwise. So, we think, what if there's a reason we are what we are— what if celestial agency has determined it so? Should we be messing with that? The error in thinking here is clear—agency is a figment our brains rely on to manage difficulty with as little trauma as possible. That's the first thing to recognize. The second is that the role for your life has only one true agent—you.

7. Your career appears to be well established, and that's good... right?

Well, maybe that's good, sure. The question becomes, is "established" what you really want? Maybe it is, and that's cool. But if "established" means you can't reach beyond certain imposed parameters to achieve anything else that you truly want, then maybe it isn't so useful after all. Like most things, this is a personal choice and it doesn't have a right or wrong answer. But it's worth acknowledging that you may very well be "establishing" yourself out of greater achievements.

8. You are afraid of losing what you have built.

A totally legitimate fear—and one we should kick out of our perspectives as quickly as possible. The reality is, you can lose everything in a heartbeat through no fault of your own, so why allow that fear to stop you from reaching out for what you really want? This goes in the same basket as "I could die tomorrow." Yes, true: we can lose, we can die. So what? Push forward.

9. You think, "Maybe I've hit my ceiling."

The proverbial "ceiling"—so long have ye been with us, and yet so little have ye given us. I side with the late great Peter Drucker, who said (paraphrasing from his classic *Harvard Business Review* article,

"Managing Oneself") if you reach a point in your career where you think you won't progress any further, then start focusing on the next part of your life. Actually, he added, you should start thinking about the next part of your life well before you begin it. The point is, forget about ceilings and focus on achievement. When you start using the cultural bugaboo of the ceiling as an excuse, you are achieving nothing and will continue to do just that.

10. Confusion about where to go.
Of all of these 10 ideas, this one is to me the most difficult because it plagues me almost constantly. Gearing up the cerebral feedback loop for achievement is one thing, but without a sense of focus and direction, all of that energy isn't going to yield very much in the end. My experience has been that sometimes you have to let the energy flow for a while without too firm a sense of direction and see if focus emerges organically. Once it does, you can then nurture it into a more structured method for getting where you want to go.

> **BCP: Think through the 10 reasons why people often fail, and determine which one or more applies to you. Adjust your adaptive thinking accordingly.**

20. Keep Tabs on Your Chemical Thresholds, Particularly Alcohol

THE SWAY OF ALCOHOL OVER MANKIND IS UNQUESTIONABLY DUE TO ITS POWER TO STIMULATE THE MYSTICAL FACULTIES OF HUMAN NATURE, USUALLY CRUSHED TO EARTH BY THE COLD FACTS AND DRY CRITICISMS OF THE SOBER HOUR.

—*William James*

What happens once that vodka cranberry works its way through your bloodstream and hits the control center behind your eyes? We hear many different things about how alcohol affects the brain and body, most notably that it is a depressant. That's only part of the story. Alcohol is a depressant, but it's also a sort of indirect stimulant, and it plays a few other roles that might surprise you.

Alcohol directly affects brain chemistry by altering levels of neurotransmitters—the chemical messengers that transmit the signals throughout the body that control thought processes, behavior, and emotion. Alcohol affects both "excitatory" neurotransmitters and "inhibitory" neurotransmitters.

An example of an excitatory neurotransmitter is glutamate, which would normally increase brain activity and energy levels. Alcohol suppresses the release of glutamate, resulting in a slowdown along your brain's highways.

An example of an inhibitory neurotransmitter is GABA, which reduces energy levels and calms everything down. Drugs like Xanax and Valium (and other benzodiazepines) intensify the effects of GABA, resulting in sedation. Alcohol does the same thing by increasing the effects of GABA. This, by the way, is one reason you don't want to drink alcohol while taking benzodiazepines; the effects will be amplified, and that can slow your heart rate and respiratory system down to dangerous levels.

So what we just discussed accounts for the depressant effects of alcohol: it suppresses the excitatory neurotransmitter glutamate and amplifies the effect of the inhibitory neurotransmitter GABA. What this means for you is that your thought, speech, and movements are slowed down, and the more you drink the more of these effects you'll feel (hence the stumbling around, falling over chairs, and other clumsy things drunk people do).

But here's the twist: alcohol also increases the release of dopamine in your brain's "reward center." The reward center is the same combination of brain areas (particularly the ventral striatum) that is affected by virtually all pleasurable activity, including hanging out with friends, going on vacation, getting a big bonus at work, ingesting drugs (like cocaine and crystal meth)—and drinking alcohol.

By jacking up dopamine levels in your brain, alcohol tricks you into thinking that it's actually making your feel great (or maybe just better, if you are drinking to get over something emotionally difficult). The effect is that you keep drinking to get more dopamine release, but at the same time you're altering other brain chemicals that are slowing and dulling you.

Research suggests that alcohol's effect on dopamine is more significant for men than women, which may account for men drinking more than women on average. According to results from the 2001–2002 National Epidemiologic Survey on Alcohol and Related Conditions (NESARC), alcoholism affects men more than women: about 18 percent of men, compared to 8 percent of women, become alcoholics over the course of their lifetime.[23]

Over time, with more drinking, the dopamine effect diminishes until it's almost nonexistent. But at this stage, a drinker is often "hooked" on the feeling of dopamine release in the reward center, even though they're no longer getting it. Once a compulsive need to go back again and again for that release is established, addiction takes hold. The length of time it takes for this to happen is case-specific; some people have a genetic propensity for alcoholism, and for them it will take very little time, while for others it may take several weeks or months.

Here's a quick summary explaining how alcohol affects different parts of the brain:

Why drinking makes you less inhibited
Cerebral cortex: In this region, where thought processing and consciousness are centered, alcohol depresses the behavioral inhibitory centers; it slows down the processing of information from the eyes, ears, mouth, and other senses; and it disrupts thought processes, making it difficult to think clearly.
Why drinking makes you clumsy
Cerebellum: Alcohol affects this center of movement and balance, resulting in the staggering, off-balance flounce we associate with the so-called falling-down drunk.
Why drinking increases sexual urges but decreases sexual performance
Hypothalamus and pituitary: The hypothalamus and pituitary coordinate automatic brain functions and hormone release. Alcohol

depresses nerve centers in the hypothalamus that control sexual arousal and performance. Although sexual urge may increase via disinhibition, sexual performance decreases.

Why drinking makes you sleepy

Medulla: This area of the brain handles such automatic functions as breathing, consciousness, and body temperature. By acting on the medulla, alcohol induces sleepiness. It can also slow breathing and lower body temperature, which can be life-threatening.

BCP: As should be clear after reading this tool, alcohol profoundly affects your brain, and consequently your thinking processes. While that isn't headline news, knowing exactly what's going on when you've had a few too many will hopefully give you pause before doing so.

21. Make a Study of People Who Love What They Do

AN UNFULFILLED VOCATION DRAINS THE COLOR FROM A MAN'S ENTIRE EXISTENCE.

—Honoré de Balzac

Some people just seem to love what they do. Sure, they have days where they'd rather be doing something else—just like everyone—but overall they are synced with their work in a way many others envy. This tool is all about examining some of the reasons these folks love what they do, so we can draw out a few practical lessons to put to use.[24]

They seldom feel disconnected from the challenge that first engaged their interest.

This understanding jumps out at me like a spider monkey every time I speak to people who genuinely love what they do. Though their career paths may have swerved here and there, they've remained connected to the initial challenge—that all-important motivating "juice"—that compelled them toward their field. Sure, at times it's harder to focus, because all of us wade into murky waters now and again, sometimes deep enough that we seem to be "losing the plot," to borrow an English phrase. But people who love what they do never fully lose sight of the challenge and the sense of purpose that drives them; they fight their way back toward it no matter how murky things get, because it's the very thing that gets them up in the morning.

They're remarkably well attuned to the "early years."
I wish that more people would realize that if they dig way back into their personal histories (and I mean way back, well into childhood), they'll connect up with some extremely important reminders. Memory is an odd beast to be sure, and cognitive science tells us that all of us "confabulate" memory to varying degrees (that is, our brains reconstruct memories, combining shards of what actually happened with bits and pieces of imagined realities). While we can't change how our brains work—and we cannot change the fact that memory is a reconstruction—we can dig like miners searching for even faint memories of what once fueled our passions.

People who genuinely love their jobs have done this—in fact, they're usually doing it all the time—and are in touch with that kid who loved to write, or tell stories, or envision amazing buildings. The important part: what these people are doing in their jobs now may not be (and usually is not) a carbon copy of those passions, but they've successfully integrated elements of those passions into what they do. In effect, they're energized kids with the seasoned perspective of adults—and that's a great place to be.

They are "portfolio" thinkers.
Psychology research, using the vernacular of business, has made an important contribution to understanding how to effectively manage loss and failure—and it has everything to do with what's in your personal portfolio. When we speak of stock portfolios, we're talking about something that is neither consistently good nor bad; it's a

mixture of ups and downs. A down cycle doesn't kill the portfolio—though it may weaken it for a time. And an up cycle doesn't make the portfolio a permanent success—though it may get it a bit closer to that goal. Portfolio thinkers know that their careers will always combine positives and negatives. The crucial thing is, they don't choke on the negatives and they don't get too high on the positives. They ride the waves of both, and by doing so they navigate their way closer and closer to what they want. If you want to love what you do, that sort of balanced, even-keel perspective isn't optional.

They don't care what you think.
Not to sound snarky, but the truth is that people who genuinely love what they do don't allow others to talk them out of it. Imagine someone who all her life wanted to work with animals in some way, maybe as a trainer, or researcher, or veterinarian—just in some way, because that's the "juice" that compels her. And then one day in school along comes an allegedly knowledgeable career counselor who tells this person that, while it's "nice" to dream about working with furry woodland creatures, the reality is that pursuing a career along those lines is fanciful. Consider practicality, consider the hard-and-fast realities of life—consider everything else except the juice.

Too bad most of us, particularly back in school, didn't have the gumption and wherewithal to tell that person, "Thanks, but no thanks—I'll take the juice." Those of us who make it through those impasses, past all the guardian naysayers, are much more likely to love what we do than those talked into a contrived conventionality. But the good news is, even if we took bad advice back then, there are still opportunities afterward to get back to what fuels our passions. It won't come easy, but precious little worth having ever does. To put a psychological bead on this observation: people who love what they do are self-actualized in the best sense of the term.

They are born succession planners.
I've spent most of my adult life in corporate environments and have no major complaints about that—but I also have no qualms about

really disliking corporate-speak; nevertheless, some corporate-isms are quite important, and "succession planning" is one of them. It simply means that for every person deeply synced into his or her position, there's another person in training to do that job when the time comes. And the time always comes eventually, because things change all the time; that's the one constant we can all be sure of.

People who love their jobs not only know this, they embrace it wholeheartedly and actively look for others to share their passions with, in hopes that they'll want to do that job one day as well. These folks aren't doing this because the company handbook tells them to— they do it because they love what they do, and that passion compels them to share their knowledge and acumen with others. And if the would-be successor isn't passionate about that position, people who love what they do take pains to help them figure out what position will fuel their motivation—because success is unabashedly addicted to creating success.

They will stay . . . but just know they'll also leave.

Why will they leave? People who love what they do recognize that organizations are important. After all, organizations often provide the infrastructure to do what fuels their fire. But no single organization has a monopoly on providing that fuel. And people who love what they do recognize that if a company or firm or nonprofit—whatever— ceases to provide an adequate venue for doing what they love, then it's time to move on. I'd like to say "It's not personal," but the truth is, it's extremely personal. It couldn't be more so. A full commitment to doing what one loves is among the most personal parts of one's life. Passion always supersedes the functionality of infrastructure and organization, and that's part of what makes it such an essential part of who we are.

They won't be stopped.

I have lost count, seriously, of how many managers I've watched try to talk a passionate person out of pursuing a path toward the thing that fulfills him or her. The manager has a plan, and this person needs to fill a prescribed role in that plan, period. But for passion-driven people who love what they do—or are trying to connect up with what they love to do—that plan will receive their deference for only as long as it takes them to navigate around it. Put another way, when a manager says, in so many words, "This is your role in my plan, and failure to fill it will have negative consequences," the smart person usually obliges, at least temporarily. But passion-driven people bent on doing what they love are already figuring out how to blow the walls off that plan and move on. You can't hold them back. Just try it and see what happens. Passion-fueled tenacity will win in the end, even if it means taking some hard knocks in the short run. Amen.

They draw people to them without even trying.
If you'll excuse the cliché—passion sells. Well, it does. People want to be around people who are passionate about what they do, because it's an infectious feeling. Take the hypothetical person who loves what he does and exudes a passion about how connected he is with the challenges of his day. Now place him among a group of people far less directed, far less passionate, and frankly a little confused about why what they do means anything at all.

Some of those people are probably so jaded that no one is going to change their perspective, but others are going to take notice. And when they get a taste, they'll want a bigger taste—and pretty soon, even if they aren't exactly sure why, they'll start feeling a strange, uplifting sensation about coming to work. That's the infection of passion, and if you've ever worked somewhere without at least a little bit of it to go around, you already know how vapid and miserable the days seem. People who love what they do pass along what psychologists call "psychosocial contagions," and just a few drops can change an office for the better. As this happens, those doing the infecting are affirmed by the infected, and a positive cycle begins.

They live in the now.
People who love what they do are not shortsighted thinkers, but they're also not going to wait around too long to see if "the pieces

come together" or whatever other euphemism you want to insert for quasi-hopeful thinking. Sure, they'll give it some time—if anyone knows, they know it takes time to pursue one's vision of fulfillment. Nothing just happens without work and time, and more work. But if you think you're going to convince genuinely passionate people that an array of external forces must align before they can act, you're wasting your time. The "now" for people who love what they do is precious, because it can disappear in a heartbeat. And that, as it turns out, is one of the most important lessons they pass along to the rest of us.

They never, ever limit their vision to serve the interests of petty competition.
Stephen Covey famously said (paraphrasing) that highly effective people don't see the "pie" as having a limited number of pieces. Instead, they see a pie with pieces enough for everyone, and it doesn't bother them to watch others get their slice. While we cannot escape the fact that we live in a competitive culture—or that we are a competitive species, just like nearly every other species on this planet—there's quite a difference between healthy embodiment of competition and petty pursuit of selfish ends. People who love what they do are competitive. They wouldn't be able to reach their goals if they weren't. But they don't invest their time and energy in scheming and undermining; they don't try to deny the other guy his piece of pie just because that means there's one less to consume. Loving what you do—no matter how competitive you have to be to attain your goals—does not require stepping on others to get there. The folks we've been talking about in this section know that intuitively, and it's a big part of the reason they're worth writing about.

BCP: Loving what you do is largely about linking your sense of purpose and passion with work that empowers you to contribute at your highest potential.

22. Boost Your Metaphor Quotient (MQ)

AN IDEA IS A FEAT OF ASSOCIATION, AND THE HEIGHT OF IT IS A GOOD METAPHOR.

—*Robert Frost*

Let's say that you and I are comparing cities we have visited or would like to visit, and I mention one that I have not yet been to but you have. You say, "It's a massive, stinking cesspool filled with garbage and crawling with every form of filth imaginable." Immediately my mind conjures an image of a filthy retention pond covered with scum, loaded with trash, and lousy with rats and roaches.

It's debatable how accurate your metaphor is, but in the moments we are speaking this doesn't really matter. What matters is that you have provided the metaphorical rudiments for me to construct an image that is now schematically associated with the city in my mind. One day I may visit that city and determine that your metaphor was inaccurate, or I may conclude that it was dead-on right. Until then— or until I come across information that contradicts or verifies your description—the image will be there. And even after that, I'll find removing that image from my mind very difficult.

That is the power of metaphor—a power so subtle we barely notice how much it impacts our thinking. Researchers Paul Thibodeau and Lera Boroditsky of Stanford University demonstrated how influential metaphors can be through a series of five experiments designed to tease apart the "why" and "when" of a metaphor's power.[25] First, the researchers asked 482 students to read one of two reports about crime in the city of Addison. Later, they had to suggest solutions for the problem. In the first report, crime was described as a "wild beast preying on the city" and "lurking in neighborhoods."

After reading these words, 74 percent of the students put forward solutions that involved enforcement or punishment, such as building more jails or even calling in the military for help. Only 25 percent suggested social reforms such as fixing the economy, improving education, or providing better health care. The second report was exactly the same, except it described crime as a "virus infecting the city" and "plaguing" communities. After reading this version, only 56 percent opted for great law enforcement, while 44 percent suggested social reforms.

Interestingly, very few of the participants realized how affected they were by the differing crime metaphors. When Thibodeau and Boroditsky asked the participants to identify which parts of the text had most influenced their decisions, the vast majority pointed to the crime statistics, not the language. Only 3 percent identified the metaphors as culprits. The researchers confirmed their results with more experiments that used the same reports without the vivid words. Even though they described crime as a beast or virus only once, they found the same trend as before.

The researchers also discovered that the words themselves do not wield much influence without the right context. When Thibodeau and Boroditsky asked participants to come up with synonyms for either "beast" or "virus" before reading identical crime reports, they provided similar solutions for solving the city's problems. In other words, the metaphors only worked if they framed the story. If, however, they appeared at the end of the report, they didn't have any discernible effect. It seems that when it comes to the potency of metaphor, context is king.

> **BCP: As this research example shows, we seldom realize how metaphors influence our thinking. Paying closer attention to how and when metaphors are being used will improve what author Daniel Pink calls our "MQ."[26] This helps us identify how we're being influenced, and how to gain greater control over our thinking and potentially our behavior.**

23. Increase Your Culture Dosage

ART IS THE IMPOSING OF A PATTERN ON EXPERIENCE, AND OUR
AESTHETIC ENJOYMENT IS RECOGNITION OF THE PATTERN.

—*Alfred North Whitehead*

What I like about Norwegian researchers is that they always seem to be trying to figure out what makes us more satisfied with life. In one study, published in the *Journal of Epidemiology and Community Health*, a team of Norwegian researchers kept tabs on roughly 50,000 men and women to assess life satisfaction, perceived state of health, anxiety, and depression.[27]

Overall, both men and women who participated in cultural activities—including playing an instrument, painting, going to the theater, and visiting museums—had lower levels of anxiety and depression, reported more life satisfaction, and generally "felt better" than those not participating in cultural activities.

But the biggest beneficiaries were men. And here's the strange part: men more interested in viewing culture—in museums and art galleries, for example—enjoyed the greatest benefits of all, even more than men actively participating in cultural and creative activities.

Odd as that may sound, it's actually a well-evidenced result. Several studies from the early 1990s onward have shown that exposure to art strongly correlates with lower anxiety and depression. (In other words, you don't have to learn to play the piano, you can merely listen to the piano to get the anti-anxiety/anti-depression benefits.) A study published in the *Journal of Neuroscience* showed that hospitalized psychiatric patients required less anxiety medication when they were regularly exposed to visual art (the result was tracked through nurses who administer the meds—right from the source, so to speak).[28]

These and other convincing results make a case that art has a quite tangible health value, even apart from the qualities we admire and value for more obvious reasons. The second study I mentioned above took the added step of quantifying how much money could be saved on meds and nurses' time using the art-exposure method, and came up with an estimated savings of $30K a year per patient.

It's worth noting that the Norwegian study also showed that the bigger the cultural dose, the more benefits one receives—suggesting that when you next visit a theater, museum, or art gallery, you'd be wise to breathe deep and dose big.

> **BCP: Both men and women benefit from regular doses of culture, and it seems that especially for men, the bigger the dosage the better. This is a tool that you can start taking advantage of right away to improve life satisfaction; no reason to delay.**

24. Begin an Enriching Routine of Reading Challenging Literature and Watching Challenging Movies

A TRULY GOOD BOOK…TEACHES ME BETTER THAN TO READ IT. I MUST SOON LAY IT DOWN AND COMMENCE LIVING ON ITS HINT.…WHAT I BEGAN BY READING, I MUST FINISH BY ACTING.

—Henry David Thoreau

This tool is a prelude to *Part III: Expand.* In that part of the book you'll find a selection of both fiction and movies that will amplify topics we've been discussing throughout the book.

But when you read challenging fiction or watch well-made movies, the messages are received more powerfully, because they aren't delivered with an intellectual syringe—they move you both intellectually and emotionally.

It is useful to engage this tool as part of your "routine"—in the best sense of the word. Make it a regular part of your day; particularly reading, since you can read during lunch breaks, before work, after work, before bed, or whenever you can make time.

BCP: This is a "just do it" tool. Check out *Part III: Expand* for some good places to start.

25. Think … *Really* Think … About Achievement and Your Effect on Others

HAPPINESS LIES NOT IN HAPPINESS BUT ONLY IN THE ATTEMPT TO ACHIEVE IT.

—Fyodor Dostoevsky

The intersection between drive and respect is important, because we all know people who are highly driven to achieve but think nothing of running over others along the way. And, we know examples of people who are respected but stagnant. This tool provides a few different ways to think about achievement, from the vantage point of achieving what you want and keeping the best interests of others in mind at the same time.[29]

Tempered Tenacity
Respected achievers are incredibly tenacious. They do not allow obstacles to stop them, at least not for long, chiefly because they've trained their thinking to immediately seek out other ways of reaching a goal. To a tenaciously driven person, there is never just one way to achieve an objective, and no one will convince them otherwise. However, the sort of achiever we're talking about also keeps the well-being of others in mind, and if one of those alternate routes will result in

unnecessarily harming someone else, then that route isn't an option, period. To the respected achiever, it doesn't have to be, because they know there are other ways to get where they want to go even if it takes longer to get there.

Consistent Commitment

Another hallmark of respected achievers is that they do what they say they'll do. They don't spin out an elaborate vision, get others to buy into it, and then run off to the next big idea because it has sparked their interest more than the first. While nurturing multiple visions is fine (assuming they are manageable), respected achievers set a high standard for themselves that what they commit to do on a project, they fully intend to do, and they will make every reasonable effort to make it happen. Granted, failure or unforeseen circumstances are always a possibility, but those are the exceptions. The respected achiever's standard of following through is consistently maintained whether or not adversity materializes, and others know that when they collaborate with a respected achiever it won't be a waste of their time.

Soulful Pragmatism

Respected achievers are typically pragmatists—they focus on what works. If one approach isn't panning out, they either figure out how to tweak it in subtle or significant ways, or they abandon it altogether and adopt a different approach. Their focus is on outcomes. But implementing a pragmatic approach without being mindful of how changes will affect others isn't commendable; it's cruel. Respected achievers know this, so they balance an outcome focus with a situational awareness of the adjustments required by others, and they work with them to make those adjustments. Again, this may build a little more time into the process, but respected achievers don't value outcomes above people's lives if there is any possibility of creating a mutually beneficial arrangement. And if there is not, they take it as a personal goal to help others transition into roles that will benefit them.

Strategic Resolution

Just like anyone else, respected achievers can become negative when things aren't going well, and just like all of us, they may vent now and again about how crappy a situation is. What they do not do, however, is drop anchor in that negative place and allow their negativity to feed itself and eventually seep into the perspectives of those around them. Instead, they experience the pain, recognize that whatever caused it (business or personal) is now part of their repertoire of experience, and then they resolve to strategically move on. In this case, strategy refers to a guiding set of action steps to push forward—and it also refers to decisions about what not to do. Strategy is choice, and resolving into a strategic mindset to pull out of a negative place requires making hard choices. People view respected achievers as those willing to make the tough choices, and that carries tremendous weight in any organization.

Responsibility Ownership

One less-than-admirable trait of many driven people is that they're good at figuring out how to avoid taking responsibility for what went wrong. If that means throwing someone under the proverbial bus, so be it. Better him than me. But the respected achiever sees things differently in a couple of ways. First, if something went wrong due to a mistake made by the team, the respected achiever owns responsibility whether or not other team members do the same. Why? Because teams are essentially organizations structured to accomplish specific goals, and if those goals aren't reached, then the team (not any one person) owns the blame, because the team (not any one person) was given the responsibility to succeed. Respected achievers own their role on the team instead of trying to explain why their responsibility should be less than the others. Second, respected achievers are intuitively reciprocal people—they treat others in the manner they wish to be treated. Their embodiment of the "Golden Rule" is not situational; it's a consistently applied maxim that guides their behavior.

BCP: You can be achievement-minded and keep the best interests of others in mind simultaneously. As you train your adaptive thinking to set and achieve goals, keep this tool in mind.

26. Understand the Elements of Self-Regulation to Improve Performance

HAVING AWARENESS GIVES US CHOICE TO MAKE A CHANGE.

—Daniel J. Siegel

Mastery of a skill comes with consistent and deliberate practice over time. But research on practice that continues after a skill is mastered suggests that practice serves another crucial purpose as well— thinking efficiently.

The study, led by University of Colorado Boulder Assistant Professor Alaa Ahmed, focused on how research subjects learned particular arm-reaching movements using a robotic arm. Participants used a joystick on the arm to control a cursor on a computer screen. Each person started from a set position to reach for a target on the screen, using both inward and outward arm movements.[30]

Participants had to exert more energy in some of the arm movements when the robotic arm created a "force field," making subjects push harder as they steered the cursor toward the target.

The test subjects first performed a series of 200 reaching trials with no force field, then two sets of 250 trials each when pushing back against the force field. The experiment ended with another 200 trials with no force field. A metronome was used to signal the test subjects to move the robotic arm every two seconds toward the target during the trials.

The first result was, as predicted, that with repeated practice the participants learned how to move the robotic arm against the force fields and reach the target with fewer and fewer errors, until they were nearly error free.

The next result, also predicted, was that even after participants had significantly reduced errors, more practice also reduced how much energy their muscles required to complete the tasks.

The clincher result, however, was that even after muscle activity stabilized (in other words, participants' muscles reached an optimum energy consumption point that required less energy to complete the same tasks), energy consumption still decreased with more practice. By the end of the study, participants who had mastered the skill and continued to practice experienced a 20 percent reduction in energy consumption. That result suggests something new about how bodies exert energy. Conventional thinking is that "metabolic cost" is a direct result of biomechanics (muscle activity); to become more energy efficient, you train your muscles to accomplish more with less.

But this study suggests that there's a wild card in the energy consumption game: *more-efficient thinking*. Neural processing and biomechanics both appear to be responsible for energy efficiency. As participants' thinking improved with practice—even after optimal muscle function was achieved—they expended less energy.

> **BCP: Energy efficiency is a mind-muscle combo. Thinking isn't just about "head stuff"—it can improve physical performance as well.**

27. Move Your Body to Manage Your Mind

ALL TRULY GREAT THOUGHTS ARE CONCEIVED WHILE WALKING.

—*Friedrich Nietzsche*

I'm not much of a runner, but for years I've watched friends who run daily reap undeniable benefits—both physically and mentally. At the same time, research has been mounting that indicates exercise overall, and running in particular, is mighty good for your brain. A study from Cambridge University and the U.S. National Institute on Aging adds to that argument, and personally I've found it difficult to ignore.[31]

What makes running such a potent cerebral enhancer is its ability to spark *neurogenesis*: the growth of new brain cells. How it does this is still a mystery. It could be because exercise increases blood flow, or limits the production of stress hormones such as cortisol, or some combination of reasons. However it happens, running could be a better antidepressant than anything you'll get from a pharmacist.

Depression is linked to reduced neurogenesis, and it's possible that SSRI drugs like Prozac encourage the growth of new brain cells. Recent research on running indicates that it does the same thing, but on an even larger scale and without the infamous side effects of the drugs, such as weight gain and decreased sex drive.

The Cambridge study used mice to demonstrate how running beefs up the memory centers of the brain. Neuroscience researchers put one group of mice on a training regimen of running on a wheel up to fifteen miles a day. The other group did nothing but nibble on carrots, wander around their cages, and poop (the rodent corollary of a typical human office job).

Both groups were then periodically put in front of a computer screen showing two identical squares side by side. When the mice nudged the left square, they received a sugar pellet reward. When they nudged the right square, they received nothing. The mice had to remember which square yielded a reward.

The results: the running group scored nearly twice as high on the memory test as the sedentary group. To make it even more interesting, the researchers moved the squares closer and closer until they almost touched, making it harder for the mice to distinguish them. The sedentary mice got steadily worse as the squares got closer together, but the running mice continued to figure it out. Researchers even tried to fool the mice by switching the squares in front of them. The running mice still nudged the square they'd been nudging to get the treat far more often than the sedentary mice.

The mice subsequently made the ultimate sacrifice for science. Brain tissue taken from the critters showed that the running mice had grown brand-new gray matter during the experiment. Tissue from the dentate gyrus—a part of the hippocampus linked to new memory formation—showed an average of 6,000 new brain cells per cubic millimeter, totaling hundreds of thousands of new cells. Not coincidentally, the dentate gyrus is one of the few areas of the adult human brain that can grow new brain cells.

What this and a growing list of research on the topic is telling us is that running and other forms of exercise can do things for the brain we're not even sure the best of modern pharmacology can do.

BCP: Quite simply—get moving. Your brain will benefit, and so will your thinking.

28. Study the Minds of Metacognitive Pioneers

AN UNQUESTIONED MIND IS THE WORLD OF SUFFERING.

—*Byron Katie*

Great thinkers, even before the advent of modern neuroscience, have helped us understand the potency of effective thinking—particularly thinking about thinking. In this tool I am providing just a small sample list of those thinkers, and I advise you to seek them out in libraries or used bookstores or online, and give them a read. Their brilliance is as important today as when they wrote their works.

- Marcus Aurelius
- Aaron Beck
- Ernest Becker
- William James

- Karl Jaspers
- Lewis Mumford
- José Ortega y Gasset
- Bertrand Russell

And, here's a short primer on one of my all-time favorite thinkers whom I simply can't recommend highly enough:

Marcus Aurelius Antoninus (121–180 CE) was a great leader and Stoic philosopher whose words ring as true today as they did during his short tenure in antiquity. He served as the sixteenth Roman emperor until his death, and is considered the last of the "Five Good Emperors" of Rome. He was succeeded by his son Commodus, a far less benign ruler whose taste for blood was well known.

While much of his time as emperor was spent in battle, Marcus made a major impact on the study of philosophy by establishing four Chairs of Philosophy in Athens, one for each of the principal philosophical traditions (Platonic, Aristotelian, Stoic, and Epicurean). Marcus kept a journal for himself, which was later published as his "Meditations." For me, his writings are first-class vittles for the mind, and I read them often. A selection of his sayings is listed below—see if your brain can't benefit from digesting and applying the simple but striking wisdom inherent in Marcus's words.

Our life is what our thoughts make of it.

The art of living is more like wrestling than dancing.

You have power over your mind, not outside events. Realize this and you will find strength.

How much more grievous are the consequences of anger than the causes of it.

The secret of all victory lies in the organization of the non-obvious.

Such as are your habitual thoughts, such also will be the character of your mind; for the soul is dyed by the thoughts.

Begin—to begin is half the work, let half still remain; again begin this, and thou wilt have finished.

Let not your mind run on what you lack as much as on what you already have.

To understand the true quality of people, you must look into their minds, and examine their pursuits and aversions.
Where a man can live, he can also live well.
Ask—this thing, what is it in itself, in its own constitution? What is its substance and material?

BCP: Find these and other great minds, read them, read them again, and embody their wisdom to enrich your life.

29. Put Yourself Through a Catastrophic Loss Exercise

TRULY, IT IS IN THE DARKNESS THAT ONE FINDS THE LIGHT, SO WHEN WE ARE IN SORROW, THEN THIS LIGHT IS NEAREST OF ALL TO US.

—*Meister Eckhart*

This tool is probably closest to "Write Your Own Obituary" for sheer morbidity value, but as with that tool, I don't intend for this one to trigger depression; in fact, quite the opposite.

Let's start with a basic fact: every one of us will experience loss, and most of us will not escape life without at least one major loss. Loss of loved ones, of friends, of jobs and careers—all and more may visit us, and some most assuredly will. None of us knows exactly how we'll handle loss until we're faced with it.

The first time I was face to face with a great loss was the day my father died. He had a heart attack during the night and was found the following morning in bed with an anguished expression on his face that I will never forget, because each deep crease around his eyes and mouth spoke of undeniable agony. When I walked into his bedroom and saw him lying there, I was confronted with a loss exceeding any I had yet experienced in my life. I'd felt the terrible sensation before of losing loved ones, but never someone so close to me, and never with the searing emotional pain of standing right there in the presence of death.

I walked closer to him, held his hand one last time, and said the one thing that always came to mind, and still does, whenever I think about my dad: "He was a good man." I then left the room, ran into the garage, and fell into a corner sobbing and dry heaving—responses that I'd not thought of in the least; they were automatic and overwhelming.

I tell you this not because I think any amount of pre-consideration of loss will quell your emotional reaction, nor do I think it should. From a neurobiological standpoint, we grieve for a reason, and to stifle that expression of emotion isn't a good idea. But I do think that preparation for loss triggers a thinking process many of us neglect, or outright deny, because going there isn't pleasant.

The problem is, denying or avoiding mental preparation for the inevitability of loss leaves you open to psychological skewers you may not expect. Immediate and final separation from a loved one—parent, spouse, friend, or child—changes you, and without any preparation, you may find the loss opening doors into dark spaces leading down into even darker corridors that seem hopelessly endless. You may find that after the experience of tragic loss, you begin the downward spiral of losing yourself.

That doesn't have to happen, and as dire as it may sound, using metacognition to create a loss scenario in the theater of your mind can help you manage actual loss when it happens. The amount of time you spend thinking through possible loss is case-specific. Whether you spend just a few minutes or an hour, the important takeaway is that you work through the various dimensions of loss—from the initial shock to managing grief. While it's impossible to exhaustively grasp loss before experiencing it, it is possible to get in touch with ways our life will change once loss occurs.

BCP: We can't escape loss, but we can consider how loss will affect us, and by carefully thinking through loss scenarios we can avoid worse outcomes after loss strikes.

30. Meet the 12 Metarepresentations of Mind

As we discussed in Chapter 1, metacognition doesn't operate at one level of conscious awareness, but across multiple levels of consciousness, creating metarepresentations that span the mind. In this final, expanded tool, we will meet 12 of these metarepresentations. They all correspond functionally to the roles played by our brain's prefrontal cortex, as well as metaphorically to what neuroscientist V. S. Ramachandran calls "aspects of the self."

This section builds upon a few especially notable offerings presented by leading thinkers in psychology, cognitive science, and behavioral science.

Daniel Siegel, MD offers the "Nine Prefrontal Functions" (which he also describes as the "elements of emotional well-being") that serve as a guide to understanding the roles of the prefrontal cortex:[32]

1. Bodily Regulation
2. Attuned Communication
3. Emotional Balance
4. Response Flexibility
5. Fear Modulation
6. Empathy
7. Insight
8. Moral Awareness
9. Intuition

Neuroscientist V. S. Ramachandran offers the "Seven Aspects of Self" that serve as a guide to understanding the dimensions to the "I" within our brain:[33]

1. Unity
2. Continuity
3. Embodiment
4. Privacy

5. Social Embedding
6. Free Will
7. Self-Awareness

Psychologist and educational specialist Howard Gardner offers elements of the "Five Minds for the Future" that embody crucial metacognitive abilities:[34]

1. The Disciplined Mind
2. The Synthesizing Mind
3. The Creating Mind
4. The Respectful Mind
5. The Ethical Mind

Conceptual thinking expert Edward de Bono offers the "Six Thinking Hats" that functionally break out thinking styles that correlate with metacognitive categories:[35]

1. White: objective
2. Red: emotional
3. Black: cautious
4. Yellow: positive
5. Green: creative
6. Blue: organizing

The grandfather of Cognitive Behavioral Therapy, Aaron Beck, offered the five elements of the mind's "Internal Control System," which are indispensable roles of metacognition:[36]

1. Monitoring
2. Appraisal
3. Evaluation
4. Warning
5. Instruction

With these and other offerings synthesized into compatible descriptions, the 12 Metarepresentations of Mind are:

1. The Journalist

Investigates, asks the hard questions, and relies on credible sources to find answers.

2. The Engineer

Designs and manages feedback loops.

3. The Governor

Regulates the reward center; manages emotional processing.

4. The Navigator

Scouts the perimeter of conscious awareness; circumnavigates unconscious barriers.

5. The Storyteller

Writes our ongoing self-narrative; manages self-image.

6. The Simulator

Uses mental representations to create meaning.

7. The Advisor

Troubleshoots problematic automatic thoughts; provides "inner voice" support in decision making.

8. The Director

Focuses and guides attention.

9. The Technician

Makes best use of external feedback technologies.

10. The Collaborator

Extends the self into interpersonal relationships; synergizes with other minds.

11. The Guardian

Protects the self from trust infringements.

12. The Creator

Extends the self into tangible external expression.

As with any metaphorical template, these descriptions are not meant to be exhaustive—nor could any hope to be. Instead, they are composite constructions erected from a vast literature on the mind's remarkable capacity to exercise what psychologist Nicholas Humphrey calls "sentition"—privatized expressive activity of the mind *as monitored by the mind*.[37]

KNOW

DO

EXPAND

EXPAND

THE LIBRARY OF THE MIND

LEARNING NEVER EXHAUSTS THE MIND.

— *Leonardo da Vinci*

THIS SECTION of the book is truly open-ended. My intention is to provide the rudiments of a multimedia library that underlies, reinforces, and extends the first two sections: *Know* and *Do*. The purpose of *Expand* is exactly what it sounds like—to expand knowledge boundaries and open new pathways, the limits of which are solely dependent upon the reader's willingness to invest time and energy in what I believe is a lifelong and edifying exploration that will change the way you think, and—I can confidently say without hyperbole—change your life.

I've broken out **Expand** into three categories:

- **Nonfiction Books** (a portion of which are described in some detail; others are provided in bibliography format)

- Fiction and Memoirs
- Movies

The Expand Library of Great Nonfiction Reads

The Brain That Changes Itself: Stories of Personal Triumph from the Frontiers of Brain Science
Norman Doidge, MD
Viking (2007)
Norman Doidge wrote one of the first popular overviews of brain plasticity research, and it still remains among the best on the shelf addressing this exciting topic. The brilliance of Doidge's work is that he makes extremely complicated neuroscience concepts relevant in ways you wouldn't expect. I continue to go back to Doidge for elaboration on brain plasticity, even as a flood of neuroscience books are published each year.

Change Your Thinking: Overcome Stress, Combat Anxiety and Depression, and Improve Your Life with CBT
Sarah Edelman, PhD
Da Capo Press (2007)
For a practical, grounded guide to understanding Cognitive Behavioral Therapy (CBT), I have found none better than Edelman's well-written, accessible book. Without getting lost in psychological jargon, Edelman provides both the underlying rationale for each step in CBT, and "how-to" approaches with expected outcomes. I refer to this book repeatedly.

The Conquest of Happiness
Bertrand Russell
Liveright (1971)
Bertrand Russell was, and continues to be, one of the most influential Western philosophers of the past century. In this book, first published in 1930, he takes a break from his work as a logician and turns his

powerful perception on a topic that affects us all. The result is, in my opinion, one of the most compelling books ever written on happiness.

Consciousness Explained
Daniel C. Dennett
Little, Brown and Company (1991)

In one of the most comprehensive attempts at explaining the phenomena of consciousness ever written, philosopher Daniel Dennett provides insights that began bridging the gap between a conceptual and a neurobiological understanding of the human mind. This remains a solid go-to book for anyone interested in the paradox of consciousness.

The Developing Mind: How Relationships and the Brain Interact to Shape Who We Are (Second Edition)
Daniel J. Siegel, MD
The Guilford Press (2012)

It is no exaggeration to call *The Developing Mind* a masterwork. Dense with insight from one of the leading thinkers in the field, this book is an opus that covers more ground concerning the conscious and unconscious mind than any other I've come across. Siegel makes a compelling argument that our minds are only in part what our brains and nervous systems do—they are also the result of interaction with other minds and external influences. While this book will strike some as "academic" in its heft, I recommend it to anyone who is seriously interested in expanding their knowledge of all matters of the mind.

Drive: The Surprising Truth About What Motivates Us
Daniel H. Pink
Riverhead (2009)

Run-of-the-mill discussions of motivation can't compare with Pink's novel approach to the subject. Author of the best-selling *A Whole New Mind*, Pink is a master at introducing readers to a different perspective, and his ideas are always worth considering.

Finding Flow: The Psychology of Engagement with Everyday Life
Mihaly Csikszentmihalyi, PhD
Basic Books (1997)
Few books are as essential as *Finding Flow* (a condensed, more accessible version of Csikzentmihalyi's magnum opus, *Flow*) when it comes to applied psychology. The principles of "flow" are integral to multiple schools of psychological thought, including CBT and flavors of creativity therapy. The term "flow" is itself a household word (as in, "When I'm writing I'm in a state of flow," meaning an uninterrupted state of focused energy during which time seems to fly by). If you haven't read this book, put it near the top of your list.

Five Minds for the Future
Howard Gardner
Harvard Business School Press (2009)
Gardner, originator of the multiple intelligences theory, does, in this short book, a tremendous job of identifying the critical thinking abilities required for leaders now and going forward. It's a quick, incisive read that is tailored for the business market, but could belong just as easily in psychology and education.

The (Honest) Truth About Dishonesty: How We Lie to Everyone— Especially Ourselves
Dan Ariely, PhD
Harper (2012)
Dan Ariely, masterful researcher and communicator, has written a book that will make you uncomfortable—and that's a good thing. Ariely skillfully pulls the veil off our conscious and unconscious tendency toward outward- and self-deception. One of the remarkable takeaways from this book is how seldom we realize that we're lying to ourselves. Perhaps it will rattle your cage a bit, but don't deny yourself the opportunity to open your eyes by reading this book. Trust me.

How to Create a Mind: The Secret of Human Thought Revealed
Ray Kurzweil
Viking (2012)

In this attempt at reverse-engineering the brain to uncover its govern-ing principles, Kurzweil takes a significant step forward in advancing the ultimate aims of artificial intelligence. More than that, however, I think Kurzweil's major contribution is in revealing and elucidating fur-ther one of the brain's chief functions as a pattern-detection machine that ceaselessly evaluates and categorizes patterns in our environment to facilitate daily adaptation. It remains to be seen whether the work the author positions in *How to Create a Mind* will one day lead to the development of a fully functioning artificial brain, but the exploration is valuable in its own right.

I Am a Strange Loop
Douglas R. Hofstadter
Basic Books (2007)

I'm hesitant to use the word "love" with respect to any book, but in the case of *I Am a Strange Loop* I'll gladly dispense with my reticence. I love this book. Not fully science, or philosophy, or literary prose—it is all, and it is more. Some 400-plus pages of genius, this is a work that will stand the test of time. Like Jaspers's *Way to Wisdom* or Hoffer's *The True Believer*, Hofstadter's work will be in college syllabi many years from now, and will still engage the sharpest minds. All gushing aside, this book deserves an esteemed place on your bookshelf, to be read and referenced again and again.

Louder Than Words: The New Science of How the Mind Makes Meaning
Benjamin K. Bergen
Basic Books (2012)

Perhaps you were not aware, but there's been quite a debate for sev-eral years among those in the brain sciences about how the magic clay in our heads determines what is and is not meaningful. Put another way, why do we think anything at all has meaning? In fact, what is meaning? Bergen's work opens a new door to understanding how our brains create meaning via "embodied simulation"—which is an intriguing term referring to the brain's capacity to simulate meaning by leveraging our personal repository of experiences. Why, across so many topics, may my sense of meaning be different from yours? Assuming we're speaking the same language, the distinction occurs not in the external, verbalized references we use, but in the internal simulations our brains busily create and project in the theater of our minds. Since you and I have different repositories of experience from which to craft meaning, we may end up with radically different simulations—and, hence, differences in our verbalized output of "meaning." This is a tremendous book on every count and highly recommended.

Managing Your Mind: The Mental Fitness Guide (Second Edition)
Gillian Butler, PhD and Tony Hope, MD
Oxford University Press (2007)
In this highly accessible book that builds on the rudiments of Cognitive Behavioral Therapy (CBT), Butler and Hope provide a blueprint for altering your thinking to yield better life outcomes in a multitude of categories: relationships, careers, physical health, and others. It is a true science-help book in that the recommendations are firmly grounded in interdisciplinary research. An added benefit is that it is written as a reference guide, enabling the reader to choose any section to expand knowledge without having to read the entire work.

Mindhacker: 60 Tips, Tricks, and Games to Take Your Mind to the Next Level
Ron and Marty Hale-Evans
Wiley (2011)
Mindhacker, unlike many books in this section, is not an exploration of what is known and not known about how our minds work; it's a practical and accessible guide for changing (or "hacking") cognitive functions to improve outcomes. Not all 60 of the proposed tips, tricks, and games are applicable for everyone, and some are clearly more practical than others—but in total, the book is an excellent guide, a

handy reference you'll want to keep on the lower tier of your bookshelf for return visits.

Mindsight: The New Science of Personal Transformation
Daniel J. Siegel, MD
Bantam (2010)
In this concise, quick read, Daniel Siegel outlines the components of "Mindsight," his contribution to consciousness studies that has since become a household term in applied psychology. Unlike his much larger text, *The Developing Mind*, in this volume Siegel condenses his research into a primer anyone can dive into and understand. It stands alongside other mainstay texts as one of applied psychology's finest contributions.

Multiplicity: The New Science of Personality, Identity, and the Self
Rita Carter
Little, Brown and Company (2008)
Why does each of us think of ourself as an individual "I" when, in truth, we are several different selves during the course of any given day? Rita Carter tackles that question in what I consider the benchmark book on multiple-selves theory. Carter, a masterful explainer of complex topics, convincingly argues that what we consider to be the self is not merely one thing, though we operate under an illusion that it is.

On Being Certain: Believing You Are Right Even When You're Not
Robert A. Burton, MD
St. Martin's Press (2008)
Robert Burton effectively argues that many of our most stubborn truth stances are not really about being right, but about feeling right. He posits that neural connections between a thought and the sensation of being correct strengthen over time because the brain experiences the sensation as a reward. The longer the reward is received, the greater the reinforcement of the connection. Burton's book explains this and related issues cogently and conversationally, without glossing over evidence-based points that are often left out of less substantial books.

On Second Thought: Outsmarting Your Mind's Hard-Wired Habits
Wray Herbert
Crown (2010)
Wray Herbert was my model for how to write about psychology topics when I first started as a science writer. His clear, jargon-free prose and his attention to the finer details of research makes him a must-read for anyone interested in the topics I've discussed in this book. *On Second Thought* is a masterful exposition of the influence of heuristics on thought. I give it my highest recommendation.

The Other Side of Normal: How Biology Is Providing the Clues to Unlock the Secrets of Normal and Abnormal Behavior
Jordan Smoller
HarperCollins (2012)
If, as some science writers have speculated, we are living in "biology's century," then Jordan Smoller's book will be remembered as one of the seminal texts supporting the claim. In a witty, accessible style, Smoller explores the "nature" side of the nature-nurture equation, and does so with bleeding-edge tools of biological research. Can you tell what someone is going to do next simply by looking at her face? Are psychopaths born or bred, and does it make a difference? Is there such a thing as a natural-born "winning personality"? Smoller investigates those and a litany of other questions in a book well worth reading at least once and referring to many times after.

The Owner's Manual for the Brain: Everyday Applications from Mind-Brain Research
Pierce J. Howard, PhD
Bard Press (2006)
When it comes to exhaustive overviews of cognitive science, few compare to Pierce Howard's monumental tome. If a reader is searching for a place to begin reading about the brain, this is an excellent choice. Howard's writing is accessible to a general audience and grounded in evidence-based propositions about how the brain works.

Personality: What Makes You the Way You Are
Daniel Nettle
Oxford University Press (2007)
Quite possibly the best short book on human personality I've read; Nettle's take on the topic is succinct and well-argued. If you are interested to know more about why you are the way you are, this is an excellent, fast read to start with.

The Rough Guide to Psychology
Christian Jarrett
Rough Guides (2011)
Christian Jarrett is the writer behind the British Psychological Society's highly regarded blog *Research Digest,* where he makes the latest psychological research accessible to a large audience. This book crystallizes the best of his work and advances the goal of opening the world of psychology to readers who might have otherwise never found it.

The Saturated Self: Dilemmas of Identity in Contemporary Life
Kenneth J. Gergen
Basic Books (1991)
Kenneth Gergen was one of the earliest prophets of what we now call "multiple selves theory." His insights concerning how we adapt to multiple social and cultural dynamics via different "selves" have been confirmed by subsequent cognitive-science research. As a seminal book in the field, and still one of the best reads on the topic, *The Saturated Self* is well worth finding and devouring.

Self Comes to Mind: Constructing the Conscious Brain
Antonio Damasio, PhD
Pantheon (2010)
Many have tried to explain consciousness, but it remains the most vexing topic in cognitive science (and possibly in all of science). Antonio Damasio, one of the world's leading neuroscientists, adds his voice and estimable contribution to the discussion. An important read for

anyone interested in following the latest evidence-based thinking on consciousness.

The Self Illusion: *How the Social Brain Creates Identity*
Bruce Hood, PhD
Oxford University Press (2012)
Bruce Hood, professor of developmental psychology at the University of Bristol, marshals an expanse of research to convincingly argue that the self—while very real in our experience—is, in fact, a useful illusion, one necessitated by the brain that gives it life. But, Hood submits, it is not only our individual brains that are doing the creating, but the intersocial web of brains that constitutes much of our life experience. Our sense of self is, you might say, a group project, because it only fully develops within the social context, and that starts before we can speak a word. This book is a fantastic contribution to literature exploring why the "I" isn't experienced as a "we" in our day-to-day lives, though each of us is, in fact, a composite character operating within an intersocial narrative.

A Skeptic's Guide to the Mind: What Neuroscience Can and Cannot Tell Us About Ourselves
Robert A. Burton, MD
St. Martin's Press (2013)
Most experts in the brain sciences agree that we need to figure out what neuroscience can and cannot truly tell us about ourselves. In recent years, an academic publishing barrage focused on brain scans has sent the media—and, in turn, the public—into a wild tizzy over what these multicolor, multidimensional renderings of our brains are really revealing. An expert corrective is necessary, and Robert Burton's book is that corrective. Burton is not only among the leading thinkers in neurology, he's also an exceptional communicator with a journalist's instinct for getting the story right. This is a bellwether book and necessary reading for anyone interested in knowing the "story behind the story" of popular neuroscience.

Social Intelligence: *The New Science of Human Relationships*
Daniel Goleman
Bantam Books (2006)
Daniel Goleman, the progenitor and popularizer of Emotional Intelligence, has added a worthwhile dimension to his earlier work with this volume by interlacing research in social neuroscience and other fields. Goleman shows how psychosocial dynamics such as "social contagions," rejection, loneliness, envy, and a host of other influences shape our role in society as much as or more than tangible factors such as income, careers, and where we choose to live.

Soul Dust: *The Magic of Consciousness*
Nicholas Humphrey, PhD
Princeton University Press (2011)
Humphrey's book is a lesser-known gem that combines elegant—almost poetic—prose with solid science. It's a great find for anyone who wants to go beyond understanding what we know about the emergent properties of consciousness, and delve into the implications of this knowledge. Instead of a nuts-and-bolts rendering of the subject, Humphrey gives us something akin to a philosophical meditation on brain science. An extremely enjoyable read.

Strangers to Ourselves: Discovering the Adaptive Unconscious
Timothy D. Wilson, PhD
Belknap Press/Harvard University Press (2002)
Strangers to Ourselves may be the best lesser-known book about the human mind ever written. If you look through the notes of almost every book that delves into the consciousness paradox, you'll find references to Wilson's work. It is, in a word, outstanding. In a relatively short book, Wilson manages to break down the hard problems of consciousness into accessible chapters that you don't need a background in the field to understand. I cannot recommend this book highly enough.

Stumbling on Happiness
Daniel Gilbert, PhD
Knopf (2006)
I personally credit Dan Gilbert with being among the most proficient at making difficult topics born of complicated research accessible to a broad audience—and doing so without compromising intellectual integrity. *Stumbling on Happiness* has deservedly risen to the upper echelon of popular psychology books and more than merits being read. Gilbert's premise is encapsulated in the question: Do you really know what makes you happy? If you think you do, all the more reason to read this book.

Subliminal: *How Your Unconscious Mind Rules Your Behavior*
Leonard Mlodinow
Pantheon (2012)
Mlodinow's combination of research-based knowledge and clever delivery makes each of his books a pleasure to read, and *Subliminal* may be his best. Instead of being another dry introduction to the consciousness-unconsciousness problem, this book is a trenchant exploration into what cognitive science has revealed about unconscious influences, and why they are so difficult to identify and grapple with, even as we daily convince ourselves that we are effectively addressing them. There may be no better book available to date explaining why "we don't know what we don't know" and why that truism matters so much.

The Tell-Tale Brain: *A Neuroscientist's Quest for What Makes Us Human*
V. S. Ramachandran
W. W. Norton and Company (2011)
V. S. Ramachandran is among an elite group of neuroscientists who can communicate their knowledge as well as any science journalist. In *The Tell-Tale Brain*, he provides a thoughtfully written guide to the state of neuroscience and its future directions. He also gives us glimpses behind the curtain of his own research—studies that have

helped shape and define the field over the last two decades. There may be no better book for understanding cognitive neuroscience; this book is required reading for anyone interested in expanding the scope of his or her knowledge about how our brains work.

Think! Before It's Too Late
Edward de Bono
Random House (2010)
Edward de Bono is a tactical master in the realm of how to alter thinking patterns. Rich terms such as "mental provocation" originated with de Bono, and have since found their way into countless business and organizational seminars focused on improving how individuals and groups process difficult problems. One of my personal favorite contributions from de Bono is his assertion that "solving a problem" isn't the best use of one's time; rather, tracing the steps that led to the problem and altering them such that the problem ceases to be a problem is the preferred route.

Unconscious Branding: How Neuroscience Can Empower (and Inspire) Marketing
Douglas Van Praet
Palgrave Macmillan (2012)
In this well-researched and insightful book about the impact of neuroscience on marketing, Van Praet manages to educate without becoming an evangelist for "neuromarketing." His approach is to explain how we have arrived at a point in cultural history in which the cognitive and behavioral sciences have shaped the messages—in all of their mediated forms—that affect each and every one of us on a regular basis. It's an excellent read for non-marketers to understand the influences they face thousands of times daily.

Wellbeing: The Five Essential Elements
Tom Rath and Jim Harter
Gallup Press (2010)
The Gallup organization has spearheaded quite a bit of research on strengths, talents, motivation, and personality. I've enjoyed

several books from Gallup, and *Wellbeing* certainly deserves to be on your reading list if you want to know what survey research has to say about what makes us feel fulfilled. Unlike many other books on similar topics, this one is grounded in well-documented findings.

Who's in Charge?: Free Will and the Science of the Brain
Michael S. Gazzaniga, PhD
Ecco (2011)
What is the left-brain "interpreter"? This is the book that will tell you, written by a pioneer of split-brain research. Among other salient questions addressed in this short, sharply written book is "Do we really have free will?" Of all authors writing about consciousness today, Gazzaniga stands among those who deserve the label of "must-read" when they publish new work. This book is no exception.

Why Everyone (Else) Is a Hypocrite: Evolution and the Modular Mind
Robert Kurzban
Princeton University Press (2011)
Robert Kurzban is an evolutionary psychologist and an engaging writer. In this book, he throws light on the experience of contradiction in the human mind and effectively argues that all of us contradict ourselves, and that doing so is fundamental to how our brains work.

Your Brain Is (Almost) Perfect: How We Make Decisions
Read Montague
Plume (2007)
Read Montague was one of the first authors to write about the new advances in cognitive science that illuminate what is going on in our brains when we make a decision. His book is still a mainstay for those interested in the science of decision making.

Your Creative Brain: Seven Steps to Maximize Imagination, Productivity, and Innovation in Your Life
Shelley Carson, PhD
Jossey-Bass (2010)
I distinctly recall the solid two hours of sheer delight I experienced when I happened upon Shelley Carson's exceptional book, and since then I've returned to it repeatedly as a reference embodying more insight than I can expand upon in this space. Carson's book is not simply meant to be read—it's meant to be applied, and any lesser usage won't do it justice. Like all great science-help, this book builds its assertions from a foundation of solid research, and then lays out a structure for how to apply what we've learned. Don't bother getting it from a library unless that's your only option, because you'll find yourself wanting to write notes in the margins and dog-ear the pages almost continuously.

The Extended Expand Library of Great Nonfiction Reads

The Age of Insight: The Quest to Understand the Unconscious in Art, Mind and Brain
Eric Kandel
Random House (2012)

Anti-Oedipus: Capitalism and Schizophrenia
Gilles Deleuze and Felix Guattari
Penguin Classics (2009)

The Anxiety and Phobia Workbook (Fifth Edition)
Edmund J. Bourne, PhD
New Harbinger Publications (2011)

The Ape and the Sushi Master: Cultural Reflections of a Primatologist
Frans De Waal
Basic Books (2001)

The Art of Strategy: A Game Theorist's Guide to Success in Business and Life
Avinash K. Dixit and Barry J. Nalebuff
W. W. Norton & Company (2010)

Better By Mistake: *The Unexpected Benefits of Being Wrong*
Alina Tugend
Riverhead (2011)

The Blank Slate: The Modern Denial of Human Nature
Steven Pinker
Viking (2002)

Boundaries of the Soul: The Practice of Jung's Psychology (Revised Edition)
June Singer
Anchor Books (2004)

Braintrust: What Neuroscience Tells Us about Morality
Patricia S. Churchland
Princeton University Press (2011)

Brain Gain: Technology and the Quest for Digital Wisdom
Marc Prensky
Palgrave Macmillian (2012)

Cognitive Therapy of Personality Disorders (Second Edition)
Aaron T. Beck, Arthur Freeman, and Denise D. Davis
The Guilford Press (2003)

The Conduct of Life
Lewis Mumford
Mariner Books (1960)

Consciousness: An Introduction
Susan Blackmore
Oxford University Press (2011)

Contingency, Irony, and Solidarity
Richard Rorty
Cambridge University Press (1989)

The Courage to Create
Rollo May
W. W. Norton & Company (1975)

Crucial Confrontations: Tools for Resolving Broken Promises, Violated Expectations, and Bad Behavior
Kerry Patterson, Joseph Grenny, Ron McMillan, and Al Switzler
McGraw-Hill (2004)

The Denial of Death
Ernest Becker
Free Press (1998)

Do Chocolate Lovers Have Sweeter Babies?: The Surprising Science of Pregnancy
Jena Pincott
Free Press (2011)

The Emotion Machine: Commonsense Thinking, Artificial Intelligence, and the Future of the Human Mind
Marvin Minsky
Simon & Schuster (2006)

Escaping the Self: Alcoholism, Spirituality, Masochism, and Other Flights from the Burden of Selfhood
Roy F. Baumeister
Basic Books (1991)

Evolve Your Brain: The Science of Changing Your Mind
Joe Dispenza
HCI (2007)

The Examined Life: Philosophical Meditations
Robert Nozick
Simon & Schuster (1989)

Feeling Good: The New Mood Therapy
David D. Burns, MD
William Morrow & Co. (1980)

Flourish: A Visionary New Understanding of Happiness and Well-being
Martin E. P. Seligman
Free Press (2011)

Friendfluence: The Surprising Ways Friends Make Us Who We Are
Carlin Flora
Doubleday (2013)

Getting Things Done: The Art of Stress-Free Productivity
David Allen
Viking (2001)

The Happiness Hypothesis: Finding Modern Truth in Ancient Wisdom
Jonathan Haidt
Basic Books (2005)

Healing the Angry Brain: How Understanding the Way Your Brain Works Can Help You Control Anger and Aggression
Ronald Potter-Efron, MSW, PhD
New Harbinger Publications (2012)

The Hidden Brain: How Our Unconscious Minds Elect Presidents, Control Markets, Wage Wars, and Save Our Lives
Shankar Vedantam
Spiegel & Grau (2010)

Hijacked by Your Brain: How to Free Yourself When Stress Takes Over
Julian Ford and Jon Wortmann
Sourcebooks (2013)

How the Mind Works
Steven Pinker
W. W. Norton & Company (1997)

How to Read and Why
Harold Bloom
Scribner (2000)

How to Think Like Leonardo da Vinci: Seven Steps to Genius Every Day
Michael J. Gelb
Delacorte (1998)

The Human Brain Book
Rita Carter
DK Adult (2009)

Influence: Science and Practice (Fifth Edition)
Robert B. Cialdini
Pearson (2008)

Little Ways to Keep Calm and Carry On: Twenty Lessons for Managing Worry, Anxiety, and Fear
Mark Reinecke
New Harbinger Publications (2010)

Love's Body
Norman O. Brown
University of California Press (1990)

Maps of the Mind: Charts and Concepts of the Mind and Its Labyrinths
Charles Hampden-Turner
Littlehampton Book Services (1981)

Maximum Brainpower: Challenging the Brain for Health and Wisdom
Shlomo Breznitz and Collins Hemingway
Ballantine (2012)

Meditations: A New Translation
Marcus Aurelius (translated by Gregory Hays)
Modern Library (2002)

Meet Your Happy Chemicals: Dopamine, Endorphin, Oxytocin, Serotonin
Loretta Graziano Breuning, PhD
System Integrity Press (2012)

Memoirs of an Addicted Brain: A Neuroscientist Examines His Former Life on Drugs
Marc Lewis, PhD
PublicAffairs (2012)

The Mind and the Brain: Neuroplasticity and the Power of Mental Force
Jeffrey M. Schwartz, MD and Sharon Begley
ReganBooks/HarperCollins (2002)

MindReal: How the Mind Creates Its Own Virtual Reality
Robert Ornstein and Ted Dewan
Malor Books (2008)

Mind Set! Reset Your Thinking and See the Future
John Naisbitt
Collins Business (2006)

Moral Clarity: A Guide for Grown-Up Idealists (Revised Edition)
Susan Neiman
Princeton University Press (2009)

The Naked Brain: How the Emerging Neurosociety Is Changing How We Live, Work, and Love
Richard Restak, MD
Harmony (2006)

Neural Path Therapy: How to Change Your Brain's Response to Anger, Fear, Pain, and Desire
Matthew McKay and David Harp
New Harbinger Publications (2005)

The New Executive Brain: Frontal Lobes in a Complex World
Elkhonon Goldberg, PhD
Oxford University Press (2009)

The New Psycho-Cybernetics
Maxwell Maltz, MD
Prentice-Hall (2002)

The Night Is Large: Collected Essays, 1938–1995
Martin Gardner
St. Martin's Press (1996)

The Optimism Bias: A Tour of the Irrationally Positive Brain
Tali Sharot
Pantheon (2011)

Organize Your Mind, Organize Your Life: Train Your Brain to Get More Done in Less Time
Paul Hammerness, MD and Margaret Moore
Harlequin (2011)

The Passion of the Western Mind: Understanding the Ideas That Have Shaped Our World View
Richard Tarnas
Harmony (1991)

The Path of Least Resistance: Learning to Become the Creative Force in Your Own Life (Revised Expanded Edition)
Robert Fritz
Ballantine (1989)

The Power of Resilience: Achieving Balance, Confidence, and Personal Strength in Your Life
Robert Brooks, PhD and Sam Goldstein, PhD
McGraw-Hill (2004)

Pragmatism
William James
Dover Publications (1995)

Psychosynthesis: A Manual of Principles and Techniques
Roberto Assagioli, MD
Viking Compass (1971)

The Ravenous Brain: How the New Science of Consciousness Explains Our Insatiable Search for Meaning
Daniel Bor
Basic Books (2012)

Redirect: *The Surprising New Science of Psychological Change*
Timothy D. Wilson
Little, Brown and Company (2011)

The Scientific American Day in the Life of Your Brain
Judith Horstman
Jossey-Bass (2009)

Self-Esteem: A Proven Program of Cognitive Techniques for Assessing, Improving, and Maintaining Your Self-Esteem (Third Edition)
Matthew McKay and Patrick Fanning
MJF Books (2003)

Sex, Ecology, Spirituality: The Spirit of Evolution (Second Revised Edition)
Ken Wilber
Shambhala (2001)

The SharpBrains Guide to Brain Fitness: 18 Interviews with Scientists, Practical Advice, and Product Reviews, to Keep Your Brain Sharp
Alvaro Fernandez and Elkhonon Goldberg, PhD
SharpBrains Inc. (2010)

The Social Animal: The Hidden Sources of Love, Character, and Achievement
David Brooks
Random House (2011)

Steal Like an Artist: 10 Things Nobody Told You About Being Creative
Austin Kleon
Workman (2012)

The Stuff of Thought: Language as a Window into Human Nature
Steven Pinker
Viking (2007)

SuperCooperators: Altruism, Evolution, and Why We Need Each Other to Succeed
Martin A. Nowak with Roger Highfield
Free Press (2011)

The Time Paradox: The New Psychology of Time That Will Change Your Life
Philip Zimbardo and John Boyd
Free Press (2008)

The True Believer: Thoughts on the Nature of Mass Movements
Eric Hoffer
Harper Perennial Modern Classics (2010)

The UltraMind Solution: The Simple Way to Defeat Depression, Overcome Anxiety, and Sharpen Your Mind
Mark Hyman, MD
Scribner (2008)

A User's Guide to the Brain: Perception, Attention, and the Four Theaters of the Brain
John J. Ratey, MD
Pantheon (2001)

Way to Wisdom: An Introduction to Philosophy (Second Edition)
Karl Jaspers
Yale University Press (2003)

What We May Be: Techniques for Psychological and Spiritual Growth Through Psychosynthesis
Piero Ferrucci
Jeremy P. Tarcher, Inc. (2009)

A Whole New Mind: Why Right-Brainers Will Rule the Future
Daniel H. Pink
Riverhead (2005)

The Will to Live: Selected Writings of Arthur Schopenhauer
Edited by Richard Taylor
The Continuum Publishing Company (1967)

William James: Writings 1878–1899: Psychology: Briefer Course / The Will to Believe / Talks to Teachers and to Students / Essays
William James
The Library of America (1992)

*You Are Not Your Brain: The 4-Step Solution for Changing Bad Habits,
Ending Unhealthy Thinking, and Taking Control of Your Life*
Jeffrey M. Schwartz, MD and Rebecca Gladding, MD
Avery (2011)

Your Brain: The Missing Manual
Matthew MacDonald
Pogue Press (2008)

FICTION AND MEMOIRS

I T'S IMPOSSIBLE to write a section called *Expand* that does not include an eclectic selection of works of fiction, biographies, and memoirs, for the simple reason that emotional connection with these works is arguably the most expand-enhancing dynamic any reader (and writer) could hope for. The written word has been, and will continue to be, an immensely powerful method of delivering compelling narrative. Putting the finest, truest point on it that I can: reading these books will change you in ways you won't be able to predict until you read them.

Once again, what is included here is a start—a suggested though admittedly brief docket of *Expand* sources in the realm of fiction, biography, and memoir. Any one of these works can, and hopefully will, lead you to venture into multiple brain-changing pathways. This is but a sliver of an immense, life-altering narrative universe.

Another Life: A Memoir of Other People
Michael Korda
Random House (1999)

The Atlas (travel memoir)
William T. Vollmann
Viking Penguin (1996)

The Book of Illusions (novel)
Paul Auster
Faber and Faber (2002)

Days Between Stations (novel)
Steve Erickson
Simon & Schuster (1985)

Daytripper (graphic novel)
Fábio Moon and Gabriel Bá
Vertigo (2011)

Deliverance (Tenth Edition) (novel)
James Dickey
Delta (1994)

Demian (novel)
Hermann Hesse (translated by Michael Roloff and Michael Lebeck)
Harper Perennial Classics (1999)

Elizabeth Costello (novel)
J. M. Coetzee
Viking (2003)

Every Love Story Is a Ghost Story: A Life of David Foster Wallace (biography)
D. T. Max
Viking (2012)

Heart of Darkness (Norton Critical Editions, Fourth Edition) (novel)
Joseph Conrad
W. W. Norton & Company (2005)

Infinite Jest
David Foster Wallace
Little, Brown and Company (1996)

In Search of Lost Time: Volume I, Swann's Way
Marcel Proust (translated by C. K. Scott Moncrieff)
Modern Library (1992)

Life After God (short fiction)
Douglas Coupland
Pocket Books (1994)

Logicomix: An Epic Search for Truth (graphic novel)
Apostolos Doxiadis and Christos H. Papadimitriou
Bloomsbury (2009)

Man in the Dark (novel)
Paul Auster
Henry Holt (2008)

Mao II (novel)
Don DeLillo
Viking (1991)

Maus, A Survivor's Tale I: My Father Bleeds History
Maus, A Survivors Tale II: And Here My Troubles Began (graphic
novels)
Art Spielgelman
Pantheon Books (1986, 1991)

The Name of the Rose (novel)
Umberto Eco
Warner Books (1984)

Persepolis: The Story of a Childhood
Persepolis 2: The Story of a Return
The Complete Persepolis (graphic novels)
Marjane Satrapi
Pantheon (2004, 2005, 2007)

The Prophet (facsimile of 1926 edition) (inspiration)
Kahlil Gibran
Martino Fine Books (2011)

The River of Doubt: Theodore Roosevelt's Darkest Journey (biography)
Candice Millard
Doubleday (2005)

Run With the Hunted: A Charles Bukowski Reader (fiction and poetry)
Edited by John Martin
HarperCollins (1993)

Samuel Johnson: The Major Works, Including Rasselas (essays, poems, letters, journals)
Edited by Donald Greene
Oxford World's Classics (2009)

Seize the Day (novella)
Saul Bellow
Penguin Classics (2003)

The Sunset Limited: A Novel in Dramatic Form
Cormac McCarthy
Picador (2010)

White Noise (novel)
Don DeLillo
Viking (1985)

Winter Journal (memoir)
Paul Auster
Henry Holt (2012)

EXPAND

MOVIES

EACH MOVIE has been chosen because it effectively deals with an aspect of consciousness that would be difficult to convey without images and audio enhancing the narrative. They are also well written and directed, and generally entertaining (don't worry, nothing dull and pedantic included). As with the previous parts of *Expand*, this is merely a beginning—an open door to infinitely more.

I've elaborated on the first ten on this list to provide a sense of why all of these movies were chosen, but for each one—those elaborated upon and the extended list—it's far better to watch them than to read my review or anyone else's.

Adaptation (2002)
Director: Spike Jonze
Narration narrating a narrated narrative—that doesn't come close to describing this excellent movie, but watch it and you'll understand what I mean. Consciousness comes to the fore through a looping of sub-narrations; it's hard to imagine this being pulled off any better than it is here.

Barcelona (1994)
Director (and writer): Whit Stillman

I've included this movie because the dialogue is intentionally written to expose conscious thought to a degree that's impossible to describe without watching it. The same writer/director made a movie called *The Last Days of Disco* that takes the same approach to dialogue and is thoroughly enjoyable, as is this one.

The Diving Bell and the Butterfly (2007)
Director: Julian Schnabel

When a spectacularly successful public figure loses his ability to speak or move, with the exception of blinking his left eye, we are brought into a conscious world enclosed within silence, and journey with him to discover how to interact with the world "out there" again.

Factotum (2005)
Director: Bent Hamer

Based on the work of iconic writer Charles Bukowski, this movie follows its protagonist through corridors of confusion and despair—or such they initially seem—that somehow lead to self-discovery and self-actualization. The well-written consciousness narration puts the icing on the cake.

The Grey (2011)
Director: Joe Carnahan

The main character in this movie experiences flashbacks that bridge the conscious and unconscious mind spaces, and that are masterfully illustrated onscreen. We also travel with him through a brutal battle for survival that challenges every facet of his deepest reasons for being, initially unknown to him but consciously discovered as the story unfolds.

The Insider (1999)
Director: Michael Mann

As a man deals with the fallout from making a life-altering decision that includes the loss of his family and career, we see his mindscape illustrated with beautiful precision.

The Salton Sea (2002)
Director: D. J. Caruso

Deep into a bifurcation of his personality—one that he initiated to achieve a soul-wrenching goal—a man finally loses a concrete sense of who he is, and sets out to live a new kind of life, more conscious of the possibilities than he ever was before.

The Spanish Prisoner (1997)
Director (and writer): David Mamet

Is anyone who they seem to be? As the main character winds through a labyrinth of deceptions and illusions—only slowly coming to terms with his role in a torturous power play—we're shown consciousness turned upside down through tense and tangled narrative.

There Will Be Blood (2007)
Director: Paul Thomas Anderson

I chose this masterwork because of what it *does not* tell us, forcing us to mentalize with the main character to determine his motivations beyond the obvious material rewards of becoming a successful oil tycoon.

Vanilla Sky (2001)
Director: Cameron Crowe

"The subconscious is very powerful." Indeed it is. What would you do if you could rebuild your life, little piece by little piece, in the way you wanted to live it from the beginning? You may have an answer in mind, but before you give it, you should also ask, would your unconscious allow you to run the tape just as you'd like? This movie is a combination of possible answers to both questions, stunningly rendered.

The Extended Expand Movie Library

American Beauty (1999)
Director: Sam Mendes

As Good As It Gets (1997)
Director: James L. Brooks

The Big Kahuna (2000)
Director: John Swanbeck

Brazil (1985)
Director: Terry Gilliam

Citizen Kane (1941)
Director: Orson Welles

The English Patient (1996)
Director: Anthony Minghella

Eternal Sunshine of the Spotless Mind (2004)
Director: Michel Gondry

Eyes Wide Shut (1999)
Director: Stanley Kubrick

Fight Club (1999)
Director: David Fincher

The Fisher King (1991)
Director: Terry Gilliam

Girl, Interrupted (1999)
Director: James Mangold

Good Will Hunting (1997)
Director: Gus Van Sant

Heavenly Creatures (1994)
Director: Peter Jackson

A History of Violence (2005)
Director: David Cronenberg

Kumaré (2011)
Director: Vikram Gandhi

The Life of David Gale (2003)
Director: Alan Parker

Lost in Translation (2003)
Director: Sofia Coppola

127 Hours (2010)
Director: Danny Boyle

On the Waterfront (1954)
Director: Elia Kazan

The Others (2001)
Director: Alejandro Amenábar

The Perks of Being a Wallflower (2012)
Director: Stephen Chbosky

Pontypool (2009)
Director: Bruce McDonald

The Reader (2009)
Director: Stephen Daldry

The Sea Inside (2005)
Director: Alejandro Amenábar

The Shawshank Redemption (1994)
Director: Frank Darabont

Taxi Driver (1976)
Director: Martin Scorsese

12 Monkeys (1995)
Director: Terry Gilliam

Up (2009)
Directors: Pete Docter, Bob Peterson

The Usual Suspects (1995)
Director: Bryan Singer

Warrior (2011)
Director: Gavin O'Connor

EXPAND

DEFINITIONS

IT IS NOT THAT I'M SO SMART. BUT I STAY WITH THE QUESTIONS MUCH
LONGER.

— *Albert Einstein*

THE DEFINITIONS in this section expand on terms used throughout the book, and also include new "leads" for those interested in further expanding and enhancing their knowledge of metacognition and a slew of related concepts, people, theories, and things. Consider this glossary a starting point for a wealth of additional learning.

allostasis—The tendency of a system to change in response to changing conditions in order to achieve and maintain balance (see **homeostasis**). The human brain is allostatic in that it must continually adapt to changing internal and external conditions to protect, recover, and even increase its equilibrium.

anoetic—The lowest form of consciousness, temporally and spatially bound to the present and only the present. For example, an ant responds to stimuli occurring in the present moment and is not able to self-reflect (**autonoetic** consciousness) or to refer to an internal representation generated by a stimulus (**noetic** consciousness); its responses are instinctually driven, without any form of internal, conscious reflection.

attention—The ability to focus the senses on a specific stimulus source. The human brain is able to fully focus attention on only one stimulus at a time. Focusing on multiple sources is an altered form of attention that increases error-proneness, unless one of the sources is completely routinized (e.g., driving and chewing gum at the same time).

attention density—The quantity and quality of attention paid to a particular circuit in the brain. For example, with concentrated focus and attention, the brain will start to fire neurons in new patterns. If this concentration is maintained over time, the pattern of nerve cell connections (the "circuit") will change and the new pattern will become permanent.

automaticity—The "shortcuts" used by the unconscious mind to enable action without lengthy mental processing. One example is the "snake in the road" reaction, in which we automatically jump back from a shape that resembles a snake ahead of us, before further inspection reveals that it's only a piece of rope. We do not have to think about our initial reaction because it's unconsciously triggered by a pattern our brain identifies in our environment.

automatic thoughts—Thoughts that arise from the unconscious without conscious prompting.

autonoetic—The highest form of consciousness; the epitome of self-reflectiveness and self-knowledge.

basal ganglia—A bundle of nuclei in the base of the forebrain that is primarily assigned to selecting and mediating movements.

blindsight—The ability to respond to visual stimuli without having any conscious visual experience; occurs after some forms of brain damage.

chunking—The process the brain uses to create accessible memories by extracting specific information from random data and establishing patterns in the data. A single unit of learning or memory is a "chunk."

Cognitive Behavioral Theory (CBT)—The practice of changing the way we think about the elements of our environment (stress, relationships, time constraints, addiction sources, etc.) in order to change our emotional response to those elements. This school of thought was chiefly founded by psychologist Aaron Beck.

cognitive distortions—In cognitive psychology, cognitive distortions are thoughts that are exaggerated and irrational. The process of learning the habit of refuting these thoughts is called "cognitive restructuring."

declarative metacognition—Metacognition that is focused on facts and tangible concepts, as opposed to theoretical or abstract concepts.

Dialectical Behavioral Therapy (DBT)—A form of therapy that emphasizes mindfulness (sometimes used as a synonym for metacognition) as a core concept. In DBT parlance, mindfulness helps individuals accept and tolerate disquieting emotions that arise when facing difficult situations or challenging hard-to-change habits and/or detrimental behaviors.

ego-dystonic—The state of believing automatic thoughts are not in alignment with one's sense of self.

ego-symmetric—The state of not defaulting to an ego-syntonic or ego-dystonic position when confronted with automatic thoughts, but rather seeking healthy detachment from these thoughts and potentially altering one's typical default reaction to them.

ego-syntonic—The state of believing automatic thoughts are in alignment with one's sense of self.

embodied simulation—The theory that attempts to explain what happens in one's brain via mirror neurons when observing the activity of another individual (see **mirror neurons**). The other person's activity is "embodied" in one's mind—in other words, a neuronal brain map is created that mirrors the brain map underlying the other's activity.

enculturated emotion theory—The theory that an individual's emotional awareness is in part dependent upon the cultural context in which she or he has been brought up and lives.

epistemic—Describes the feelings associated with the experience of trying to solve a cognitive task. Examples include the feeling of knowing and of forgetting, the feeling of confidence or of uncertainty, and the tip-of-the-tongue phenomenon.

exteroception—How one perceives the world outside of one's own body (contrast with **proprioreption** and **interoceptive awareness**).

feeling of knowing (FOK)—One of the two main assessments of metacognitive awareness (the other is judgment of learning: JOL) that determines the extent to which an individual *feels* that he or she can recall a specific item from memory when the item is described or otherwise pointed out. This test is not of actual recall, but of feelings about recall. For example, someone is asked to name a particular city that is known for its intricate canal system and she says she "feels like she knows" the answer; a feeling that is confirmed once Venice, Italy, is pointed out on a map. Tip-of-tongue state is an example of an FOK.

forebrain—A major part of the brain, including the cerebrum, thalamus, and hypothalamus.

Hebb's law—Named after psychologist Donald O. Hebb, this law describes the basis of neuroplasticity: "Neurons that fire together wire together." Hebb's law is central to understanding how the human brain learns new information and forms memories.

higher-order thinking (HOT)—Higher-order thinking involves the learning of complex judgment skills such as critical thinking and problem solving.

homeostasis—The state of internal balance within a system. The human brain has evolved to seek homeostasis, rather than extreme conditions such as too much or too little stress.

insular cortex—Also referred to as the "**insula**," the brain region that lies in a deep recess between the temporal and frontal lobes.

intentionality—Intentionality is the power of minds to represent, or to stand for, things, properties, and states of affairs—most specifically, the mindsets of other individuals. The "levels of intentionality" refer to our ability to assume the mindset of another person. First-order intentionality is the ability to reflect upon one's own thoughts (mindset). Second-order is the ability to assume another's mindset. Third-order intentionality is the ability to assume the mindset of someone assuming the mindset of someone else. Fourth-order intentionality is the ability to assume the mindset of someone who is assuming the mindset of someone assuming the mindset of someone else. And so forth. It is thought that only humans are cable of third-order and higher intentionality, possibly as high as sixth-order. Nonhuman primates appear to be capable of first- and second-order intentionality.

interoceptive awareness—Awareness of internal bodily functions. An "interoceptor" is a specialized sensory nerve receptor that receives and responds to stimuli originating from within the body (see also **proprioception** and **exteroception**).

introspection illusion—The illusion of believing we have gained full understanding of a dynamic occurring within the unconscious mind. By definition, we can only fully understand that which becomes conscious, or occurs within the conscious mind. Said another way, introspection is limited to conscious mind space.

ipsundrum—A term coined by psychologist Nicholas Humphrey to refer to what is created when the mind generates a hypothesized image in response to sensory stimulation of an unknown source. The hypothesized image is an "ipsundrum."

judgment of learning (JOL)—One of the two main assessments of metacognitive awareness (the other is feeling of knowing: FOK) that determines if an individual improves his or her ability to learn new information by exercising metacognition. Research indicates that merely making a positive judgment that information has been learned improves actual learning.

left-brain interpreter—A term coined by neuroscientist Michael Gazzaniga to refer to the explanations the left brain constructs in order to make sense of the world by reconciling new information with what was known before. The left-brain interpreter attempts to rationalize, reason, and generalize new information it receives in order to relate the past to the present.

metacognition—A term literally translated as "thinking about thinking" that refers to the unique human capability to reflect on thought processes from a point of mental detachment. This capability originates in the prefrontal cortex, the most recently evolved part of the human brain, which serves as the master control center for higher-order conscious thought.

metacognitive awareness—The extent to which someone has developed her or his metacognitive capability. The greater one's metacognitive awareness, the more effectively one can detach from conscious thought processes and evaluate them before moving to the next thought or behavioral step.

metaphor quotient (MQ)—A term coined by author Daniel Pink that refers to an individual's facility with understanding and crafting metaphors.

metarepresentation—The ability to visualize mental representations in the mind. Sometimes used in conjunction with the terms "Theory of Mind" and "mental theater."

midbrain—Also called the mesencephalon, it's the area of the brain between the forebrain and the brainstem involved in the control of motor functions such as eye movement and body movement, and their integration with the sensory cues of vision and hearing. Includes the basal ganglia.

mindfulness—A core concept of Dialectical Behavioral Therapy (DBT) that helps an individual observe, evaluate, and better tolerate emotional states. It's closely related to metacognition, and in some cases the terms are used interchangeably.

mindsight—According to the term's originator, Dr. Daniel Siegel, "Mindsight is the way we can focus attention on the nature of the internal world. It's how we focus our awareness on ourselves, on our own thoughts and feelings, and it's how we're able to actually focus on the internal world of someone else...it's how we have insight into ourselves, and empathy for others."

mirror neurons—A distinctive class of neurons that discharge both when one executes a motor act and when one observes another individual performing the same or a similar motor act. For example, when someone observes another person crying, mirror neurons respond by eliciting the feeling of sadness. Mirror neurons are thought to be an essential component of empathy in humans and primates.

ncoteny—The retention of juvenile characteristics in the adults of a species. Humans, for example, demonstrate neoteny by retaining into adulthood the relatively large head and hairlessness characteristic of very young primates.

neurofeedback—Information about neural functions in real time, which theoretically can be used in neurofeedback training to enable people to alter their thinking and behavioral outcomes. Similar to biofeedback, which applies the same principle to overall bodily functions. For example, when you step on a scale in the morning, you are receiving a form of biofeedback about your body. When someone undergoes an fMRI brain scan, they are receiving information via the resulting brain image about specific neural functions and how they may correlate with mental actions or feeling states.

neuroplasticity—The collection of ways in which the brain changes in response to what we do and experience. The concept of neuroplasticity is tied to the idea that we can change the way we think, and our corresponding abilities, throughout our lifetimes.

new unconscious—A term used to distinguish the "unconscious" of modern parlance from that described by Freud. Freud's definition of the unconscious is radically different from the definition typically used in cognitive science today. And while his contributions to the field were useful, Freud's concept of the unconscious is no longer considered accurate given the wealth of research conducted over the past half century.

noetic—A mid-state form of consciousness in which judgments are made about internal representations (e.g., seeing a bear triggers a previously learned internal judgment that bears are dangerous).

opponent process theory—In psychology, opponent processes are emotional reactions that counterbalance each other. For example, after acute pleasure, opponent process theory predicts that an individual will experience withdrawal (as is the case in drug and alcohol addictions). Opponent process theory in this usage is most frequently associated with the work of psychologist Richard Solomon.

prefrontal cortex—The region of the brain in the forwardmost part of the frontal cortex, involved in planning and other forms of higher-level cognition, including metacognition.

perception—The awareness or understanding of the source of sensory input (see **sensation**). Perception is a subjective ability because one person's perception of a sensory source may be different from another's. For example, if two people are walking through the woods and both hear a large rock hitting a nearby tree, one person may perceive the cause of the activity as a natural occurrence (such as rocks falling from a hillside), while the other may perceive the cause to be intentional (e.g., a bigfoot throwing a rock as a warning to the walkers).

phonemic restoration effect—A perceptual phenomenon whereby, under certain conditions, sounds actually missing from a speech signal can be hallucinated by the brain and clearly heard. The effect occurs when missing phonemes in an auditory signal are replaced with white noise, resulting in the brain filling in absent phonemes. The effect can be so strong that listeners do not even know that there are phonemes missing. This effect is commonly observed in a conversation with heavy background noise, making it difficult to properly hear every phoneme being spoken. Different factors can change the strength of the effect, including age and gender.

pragmatic adaptation—The brain's daily challenge of adapting to both the changing internal environment of the body and the external environment—including the social and cultural contexts in which one lives (also see **allostasis**).

proprioception—The sense of the relative position of neighboring parts of the body and of the strength of effort being employed in movement (contrast with **exteroception** and **interoceptive awareness**).

psychological immune system—A metaphor for the resilience of the human mind. Theoretically, the "psychological immune system" protects us from experiencing the worst possible psychological outcomes from trauma and other emotionally negative events.

quantum Zeno effect—A term originating in quantum physics (coined by George Sudarshan and Baidyanath Misra of the University of Texas in 1977) that has since been expanded and applied to neuroscience. Psychiatrist Jeffrey M. Schwartz offers this succinct definition: "The quantum Zeno effect for neuroscience application states that the mental act of focusing attention can hold in place brain circuits associated with what is focused on (e.g., pain versus pain relief). Focusing attention on mental experience maintains the brain state arising in association with that experience. What this means is that if one focuses attention on an experience, the set of relevant brain circuitry with which that experience is associated will be held in a dynamically stable state."

reticular activating system (RAS)—The area of the brain that acts as a toggle switch between the cerebral cortex and the limbic system. When the cerebral cortex is fully functional (creating, planning, problem solving), the RAS tunes down or turns off the limbic system (stress response, fight or flight), and when the brain is under extreme stress, the RAS shuts down the cerebral cortex.

science-help—A genre that focuses on usable knowledge drawn from solid, research-based findings from a range of fields, including psychology, neuroscience, economics, ecology, communications, business management, marketing, the humanities, and many others.

scripting—In psychology, scripting refers to previous learning that has become "automatic" and influences thoughts and behavior without conscious deliberation (i.e., unconsciously incorporated learning that runs like a "script" in the mind).

self-efficacy—A term generally associated with psychologist Albert Bandura referring to one's belief in one's ability to succeed in specific situations. One's sense of self-efficacy can play a major role in how one approaches goals, tasks, and challenges. The concept of self-efficacy lies at the center of Bandura's social cognitive theory, which emphasizes the role of observational learning and social experience in the development of personality. According to Bandura's theory, people with high self-efficacy—that is, those who believe they can perform well—are more likely to view difficult tasks as something to be mastered rather than something to be avoided.

self-image—The conception that one has of oneself, including an assessment of self-qualities and personal worth.

sensation—The function of the low-level biochemical and neurological events that begin when a stimulus influences the receptor cells of a sensory organ. It is the psychological state preceding perception.

sentition—A term coined by psychologist Nicholas Humphrey to refer to sensations that are monitored by one's mind. For example, when you see a red light, the internalized response to the "redness" of the light creates an internal sensation. Your mind is always monitoring these sorts of internal sensations—this monitoring activity is sentition.

set-point theory of happiness—The theory that each of us has an internal gauge for how happy we feel relative to others. For some the set point may be very high, for others low, and for most somewhere in between. Whenever we experience periods of especially high or low happiness, the set-point theory predicts that we will eventually return to our normal (internally regulated) happiness level.

signal detection theory—Refers to the ability to detect or likelihood of detecting some stimulus in proportion to the intensity of the stimulus (e.g., how loud a noise is) and your physical and psychological state (e.g., how alert you are).

survival value—The benefits of an organism's attributes and/or behavior that increase its chances of surviving and reproducing (e.g., a human's higher-order consciousness and metacognitive ability have extremely high survival value).

Theory of Mind (TOM)—The branch of cognitive science that investigates how we ascribe mental states to other persons, and how we use the ascribed states to explain and predict the actions of those other persons. These skills are shared by almost all human beings beyond early childhood. Sometimes used in conjunction with the terms "metarepresentation" and "mental theater."

tip-of-tongue state—The failure to retrieve a word from memory, accompanied by a feeling that capturing the word from memory is imminent. Tip-of-tongue state is an example of an "epistemic feeling" and an FOK, or "feeling of knowing."

APPENDICES

APPENDIX 1

WHAT IS SCIENCE-HELP?

SINCE THE PUBLICATION of my book *What Makes Your Brain Happy and Why You Should Do the Opposite*, I've often been asked to elaborate on a term I used in the book's introduction and closing chapter: "science-help."

I used the term to make a distinction between two different approaches to writing about the mind and human behavior. The word "approaches" is crucial, because I'm not really interested in categorizing types of books. Stroll through the self-help section of any bookstore and it's immediately clear that the genre is anything but homogeneous. You'll find books by motivational speakers next to books by relationship experts; salacious primers on becoming a better pick-up artist next to stoic workbooks for breaking codependences. It's difficult to identify the method used to build the section, which, at least in the larger stores, is usually quite massive.

The term "science-help" is also not a line in the sand between good and bad books. The self-help section is an expansive potpourri, and within it are books both shallow and weighty. Three of my favorite examples to illustrate this point are books I originally found in the self-help section and consider among the best on my bookshelf: *Stumbling on Happiness* by Dan Gilbert; *The Happiness Hypothesis* by Jonathan Haidt; and *Finding Flow* by Mihaly Csikszentmihalyi.

I can understand why those books are in the self-help section, but could just as easily argue that they should be in psychology. Ultimately, it really doesn't matter. What matters is that people find them and read them; how they're categorized is far less important than how they affect people's lives. And while I would not consider those books typical of the self-help section, they exemplify at least part of it—reason enough to be cautious about blanket criticisms.

What I want to convey with the term science-help is that several of us are writing books about a range of topics in psychology and cognitive science that are also applicable to daily living. To get from science to application takes a lot of work. In my case, I spent three years reading and writing about the latest research in psychology, behavioral science, and neuroscience, and spoke with leading minds in those and additional disciplines to get traction on the material. Before that I spent more than fifteen years immersed in social science research simply because I love it, even though a draft manuscript hadn't yet reached the tangibility of a daydream.

Science-help is defined by science first. Pulling applicable lessons from the science is—and should be—a conservative process. We have to be cautious about what we claim, because more often than not the lessons we offer are rooted in correlations. Many of those correlations are quite strong, but they should not magically morph into hard-and-fast causations once they find their way into a book. A "science first" approach means that we don't pretend to provide ironclad conclusions, but rather suggestions derived from the credible findings of well-structured research.

We humans are too prone to latching onto systems for better living—programs for success and happiness. Typical self-help has, for many years, provided the platform for books promoting those systems and programs, and they've surely benefited their authors far more than their readers.

Science-help takes a step back from that arena and asks, "Why are we really writing these books?" If the answer is that we want readers to benefit in the long term from the knowledge they find—not merely feel good about themselves while reading crafty empowerment prose—then it's incumbent upon the authors to do the difficult work of living the science before writing a single word.

Someone recently asked me if I thought science-help should become a new section in bookstores. It's an intriguing idea, and I don't think there'd be any problem finding books to populate the section from the get-go. Whether or not that ever happens, however, I think the more important outcome is that readers embrace the distinction and judge books in the genre accordingly.

I personally think we've had enough books about secrets and systems, and could use more rational analysis of hard scientific work. The first approach flamboyantly promises something it can't really deliver; the second promises nothing, but offers a glimpse of new understandings about human thought and behavior that may truly benefit us in the long term. That, in short, is what science-help is all about.[1]

APPENDIX 2

WHY WE NEED PRAGMATIC SCIENCE

SINCE I WRITE about science-related topics for several publications, I sometimes find myself in discussions about the role of science in finding "truth." An argument that surfaces in the more
heated of these chats is that science is an overvalued discipline—a
secular deity defaulted to by those with a dangerously inflated view of
humankind's wherewithal.

This argument comes from two sources that are in most ways polar
opposites. The first, and most obvious, is theistic. In this view, science
has become a false replacement for God. Our "faith" in science is a
flimsy proxy for faith in a higher power. Humanity was limited by its
creator from the beginning, so what makes us think we can pretend
to the throne with the trite explanatory powers of science? We may
as well be climbing the tower of Babel to shoot arrows at the sky. This
devotion to science isn't just arrogant; it's an affront to the Almighty.
Worship of reason is making us blind.

The other source is on the far side of the philosophical field from
the first: postmodern-atheistic. In this view, as with the first, humankind has replaced God with science, but since there never was a God
to begin with, Science (capital "S") is just as empty a figurehead as

what it replaced. In some ways this view is even more critical of science than theism: it paints humankind as naïvely privileging one discipline above all others in an effort to save ourselves from the plainly inevitable. Has science saved us from wars, from age-old religious conflicts, from diseases and disasters? Science can't fend off the barbarians at the gate any more than it can cure the common cold, and we barely lived through the bloodiest century in history as proof of its failures.

Both of these positions target the same foe, which I'll call the *hard position* of science, or what is popularly called "scientism." The hard position is all or nothing: either science is the highest-order discipline for uncovering the truth and showing the way to a better future, or nothing is. Science demands our respect because only it is capable of getting us where we want and need to go. It stands apart from every other conceivable route to knowledge because all the others are corrupted by varying levels of subjectivity and bias. Only the empirical route of science yields objective truth.

Before I discuss the alternative, it's important to mention that I personally don't know anyone who holds exclusively to the hard position of science, and seldom do I even read a book written from this position (with a few exceptions). Overall, it's little more than a straw man target, no more legitimate a characterization than an atheist painting all Christians as science-hating fundamentalists.

The alternative to this straw man is what I'll call the *pragmatic position* of science (I'm not going to use "soft" because it implies meanings that don't apply here). The pragmatic position, by my definition, views science as one of our best *tools* for figuring out our place in the world and our world's place in the universe. To the extent that truths can be uncovered, science is one of our most effective methods for finding them. But it's not the only one. Logic is another, as are philosophical inquiry and the humanities, among others. All of these are tools that, at their best, broaden knowledge, expand understanding, and help us determine how we can leave the world in better shape than we found it.

The pragmatic position doesn't claim for science, or for scientists of any stripe, an "objective" privilege. Paraphrasing the pragmatist philosopher Richard Rorty (who was paraphrasing Daniel Dennett), there is no magical "sky hook" available to pull anyone out of their perspective into a rarefied position of seeing things "as they truly are." Humans are bias-prone through and through, and despite efforts to assume a different perspective, we still see the world through our own eyes.

And that's exactly why we need the tool called science. You can't move a boulder alone, but with the right tools the challenge shifts from unthinkable to possible. Science is one of the best tools we have to reach beyond our limited capacity. It's not a flawless tool by any means, and it can't right all the wrongs that beset our brains. But when compared to several other modes of inquiry, it's one of the best we have.

In response to those who target the hard-position straw man, we might ask where we'd be if science wasn't in our toolbox. For example, for every disease that still plagues us, another has been cured or made less harmful through a steadfast scientific dedication to improving lives. Another example: for every species that has suffered extinction at human hands, others have been saved through dedication to better understanding the natural world and the impact of our actions.

Hundreds if not thousands of similar examples could be named, but the point remains the same: we can't rid ourselves of the problems that come with living on this planet, but having science in our toolbox gives us an opportunity to manage many of them, some of which would otherwise finish us off for certain.

Targeting the straw man generates sound and fury, but when it comes to providing concrete alternatives to the explanatory and edifying role of science, it signifies precisely nothing. If either supernaturalism or postmodernism were a reliable tool for expanding understanding and improving our lot, we'd have every reason to value them as much as or more than science—but the truth is, they're not. In fact, the absolutism endemic to both makes them philosophical cul-de-sacs.

Science, in contrast, is an open road. It's not the only road, but without it we wouldn't get very far. Indeed, we might have dead-ended already.[2]

APPENDIX 3

ON THE CHALLENGES OF SCIENCE COMMUNICATION
(or, Why Scientists and Journalists Don't Always Play Well Together)

A FEW MONTHS AGO I came across a blog post written by a well-credentialed scientist, the gist of which was that he'd recently given his last interview to a journalist. So horribly had his words been misrepresented in the subsequent article that he finally had to draw the line—he would not contribute to public science schlock ever again. He was infuriated, and with good reason: not only did the article reflect poorly on him, but the focus of the research he discussed was lost in the resulting muck.

That unpleasant thumbnail touches on a debate that has been brewing in science and journalism circles for a long time, though recently it has been percolating to the surface in blog posts, tweets, and flaming Facebook posts. And while in some sense the debate will never end (because, well, these debates never do), this one should be troubling to more than just the interlocutors involved. Science knowledge brought to the public's doorstep is colored by this debate, for better and for worse—and if you think public education is important, then you already know that the associated risks are not small.

I've spoken to people with strong feelings on both sides of this issue. While few scientists disparage all journalists, it's fair to say that the majority are generally skeptical of journalists, and journalists, while they might not like it, are used to being viewed askance by scientists.

They chalk the scientists' skepticism up to the personality of those drawn to technical disciplines. As an engineer with a penchant for harping on minor details once told me, "You know, I wouldn't have to keep correcting you if you didn't keep being wrong." That, in a nutshell, describes the alleged technical/scientific personality—at least in the view of many in the journalism world.

And if the debate were that simple, we could brush it aside as a quirky nose-thumbing match between professionals. But it's not. Harder issues are involved than personality types and tones. The biggest and, in my view, most intractable of these is mistrust.

Scientists mistrust journalists because the popular market for news can, and very often does, affect how stories are told. This is particularly true now, with the standard-bearers of traditional journalism giving way to the sprawling fragmentation of online news. Many journalists have been forced to become mercenaries in a marketplace with few empires left to retain their services full-time. The pressures working against survival in this market are severe, and time constraints to produce an enormous amount of copy in any given week are rarely flexible.

But even before this market materialized, the traditional news outlets were showing signs of slippage on fact checking and filtering sensational claims from quality content. And journalists, watching as chips of the stoic walls began crumbling, were under unmanageable pressure to produce to keep their jobs.

Scientists, as sources to journalists in the maelstrom, have become increasingly fearful that the credibility of their findings is being stretched thin to grab readers' attention. Making the news "sexy" frequently means glossing over crucial distinctions, like the classic distinction between correlation and causation (correlation is never as sexy as causation even on its best day).

As well, the ambiguity surrounding many scientific findings doesn't translate well to popular messaging. What isn't quite clear in any given research study magically becomes "A + B = C" in an article about the study. The apprehensions of the researchers about broadly applying their findings may be mentioned, but by the time a reader gets to those, the impact has already been made.

On the other side, many science journalists resent the fact that these criticisms are unfairly painted across the profession. For those of us who primarily focus on science topics, "getting it right" isn't an academic exercise, it's a heartfelt desire born of a passion for what we choose to write about. For any serious writer, not treating his or her chosen subject with the care it deserves isn't an option.

That, of course, does not mean science journalists always get it right. But the writers I regularly speak to acknowledge this fact and are just as unhappy about it as the scientists. The flip side of the coin is that some scientists are not immune to overhyping findings for a little extra ink. The perfect storm occurs when an overhyping scientist meets an imprudent journalist; shortly thereafter a story about vaccines causing autism appears, for just one example.

For a long time, many journalists would fire back at scientists by saying that without the journalists, the scientists' research would never reach anyone outside of the few who read peer-reviewed journals. This is far less true now, as many in the science community have emerged as talented communicators with the wherewithal to reach broad audiences themselves. The blogging world features many of them, as do some of the better science magazines on your local bookstores' shelves.

Thankfully, there is an attainable middle ground. Some scientists and journalists have chosen (to use a Reaganism) to "trust, but verify," and I think this is the healthiest outcome of the debate that we can hope for. Scientists have every right to be concerned about how their work is represented to the world. If they choose to extend their trust to a journalist to handle the subject well, the journalist should also be willing to reciprocate by making every effort to tell the story appealingly, but without reckless embellishment. That means checking and double-checking the facts and making sure that the scientists' reservations are honored.

Both sides have a role to play for the arrangement to work well. And when it does go well, excellent, evidence-based writing results. You only have to read the work of Carl Zimmer, Jena Pincott, Wray Herbert, Rebecca Skloot, and David Dobbs, to name just a few examples, to see what can happen when good science meets good writing.

If we are willing to extend some trust and work as partners trying to reach the same goal—thoughtful communication of important scientific findings to the public—then the science sandbox needn't be such a treacherous place to play.[3]

APPENDIX 4

HOMAGE TO THE GODFATHER OF BRAIN CHANGING: WILLIAM JAMES

WHILE IT'S DIFFICULT to single out one great mind among the many great minds that have contributed to our current understanding of the adaptive brain, this section pays homage to one of the first and most original minds to start the ball rolling—and well before neuroscience would begin producing evidence to reinforce his assertions.

William James
(January 11, 1842 – August 26, 1910)

"Human beings, by changing the inner attitudes of their minds, can change the outer aspects of their lives."

FIGURE A4.1

William James defines the term "ahead of his time." Before neuroscience gave scientific backing to concepts such as "automaticity," James was already writing about them. His astounding intuition concerning why we think as we think and act as we act has never been eclipsed, and has few parallels in any field. In addition, he is also the godfather of pragmatism—the philosophical underpinning of this book and others focused on using evidence to direct a pursuit of "what works."

What follows is a summary of James's works, provided so that you can search him out and experience his genius for yourself, if you've not done so already.

Works by William James

COLLECTED WORKS

Frederick H. Burkhardt, ed. *The Works of William James*. Cambridge and London: Harvard University Press, 1975.

William James: Writings 1878–1899. New York: The Library of America, 1992.

William James: Writings 1902–1910. New York: The Library of America, 1987.

INDIVIDUAL VOLUMES

Essays in Philosophy. Cambridge and London: Harvard University Press, 1978.

The Meaning of Truth. Cambridge and London: Harvard University Press, 1979. Originally published in 1909.

A Pluralistic Universe. Cambridge: Harvard University Press, 1977. Originally published in 1909.

Pragmatism. Cambridge: Harvard University Press, 1979. Originally published in 1907.

The Principles of Psychology, Vols. I and II. Cambridge: Harvard University Press, 1981. Originally published in 1890.

Some Problems of Philosophy. Cambridge and London: Harvard University Press, 1979. Originally published in 1911.

Talks to Teachers on Psychology; and to Students on Some of Life's Ideals. New York: Henry Holt, 1899.

The Varieties of Religious Experience. New York: Longmans, Green, 1916. Originally published in 1902.

The Will to Believe and Other Essays in Popular Philosophy, Cambridge and London: Harvard University Press, 1979. First published in 1897.

ESSAYS OF SPECIAL INTEREST

"Philosophical Conceptions and Practical Results," 1898. Contained in *Pragmatism*, pp. 255–70.

"Remarks on Spencer's Definition of Mind as Correspondence," first published in the *Journal of Speculative Philosophy*, 1878. In *Essays in Philosophy*, pp. 7–22.

LETTERS

The Correspondence of William James. Ignas K. Skrupskelis and Elizabeth M. Berkeley ed. 12 volumes. Charlottesville and London: University Press of Virginia, 1992.

The Letters of William James: Edited By His Son, Henry James. Boston: Atlantic Monthly Press, 1920.

Selected Letters of William and Henry James. Charlottesville and London: University Press of Virginia, 1997.

AFTERWORD

CIENCE writer David DiSalvo lives at the high-speed, cerebral intersection of science and culture, bearing personal testimony in print each week to the evolving realities of our global human existence. This book, *Brain Changer*, is a follow-up to his first book, *What Makes Your Brain Happy and Why You Should Do the Opposite*, and functions as a literary bridge from an old world of nebulous self-help solutions to life's problems to the new world of science-help—a term DiSalvo coined in his first book.

In *What Makes Your Brain Happy*, DiSalvo presented us with compelling scientific evidence to support the curious supposition that our brains are actually programmed by nature's evolutionary process to trip us up and fake us out with weak and erroneous solutions to life's most challenging circumstances. Worse yet, in the social context, a collective ignorance of these mental limitations—accelerated by technological innovation and progress—has resulted in a random assemblage of cultural institutions governed by rules and restraints that require more of the individual's will to comply than the human brain can handle. In short, Book I of DiSalvo's exploration is about the *problem* our brains face when confronted with cultural stimuli, and he presents the reader with an evolutionary interpretation of scientific data pointing to one unassailable fact: *the quality of human existence, and the attendant pursuit of human happiness in the wider social context, is severely hampered by the brain's biochemically predetermined default settings.*

Within the pages of *Brain Changer*, however, the author offers a plausible *solution* to this evolutionary dilemma. He introduces us to novel concepts like (1) metacognition, (2) conscious self-narrative, and (3) pragmatic adaptation to give us hope that the human brain—while biologically predisposed to laying booby traps—is a magnificent machine capable of avoiding such snares of its own design. Supporting his argument with masses of data gleaned from the pages of current scientific discovery, DiSalvo successfully convinces the reader to accept the brain's capacity to recognize its foibles and pitfalls. He simultaneously deconstructs layers of labyrinthine patterns related to interconnected systems of cultural stimulus that directly influence observable instances of self-destructive human behavior. As one reader reported his computer-savvy daughter observing, after reading through a few pages of *What Makes Your Brain Happy*: "This guy shows us how to hack our own subroutines!"

But there is a singular and serious caveat to DiSalvo's declaration of hope for our capacity to override the biologically programmed circuitry of our brains bent on self-destruction. His sole reservation lies in the all-too-human awareness that individuals must take direct action to counter their own cognitive-behavioral predilection and propensity for *IN*action.

In this vein, DiSalvo is not beyond considering the possibility that most humans are mired in the swarm of their own inertia and a natural predisposition for taking the path of least resistance to their own peril.

As Walter Lippmann observed half a century ago,

> It is all very well to talk about being the captain of your soul. It is hard, and only a few heroes, saints, and geniuses have been the captains of their souls for any extended period of their lives. Most men, after a little freedom, have preferred authority with the consoling assurances and the economy of effort which it brings.

Caution and caveats aside, DiSalvo's optimism in this volume is apparent and his solution, though grounded in hard science, rings true to the poetic yearnings of the human heart. *Know. Do. Expand.* DiSalvo exhorts his reader to take action—*informed* action—in pursuit of whatever passion a reasonable person can justify in any given cultural context.

To appreciate his own commitment to this "solution" one need only to observe DiSalvo in his natural setting. On any given day, the man can be found at his favorite corner coffee shop commandeering tabletops and wicker-bottom chairs strewn with books and stacks of research containing "burgeoning content" (as he calls it) for his next book, article, or blog post.

"In the wake of postmodernism," he tells me over the phone, while buried amid bibliographic piles of *content*, sipping his coffee, "the jury is still out on what actually constitutes a culture. But that shouldn't stop us from pragmatically adapting to meet its demands." When I ask him, "Who makes culture?" he pauses briefly and responds, "I think it's quite clear who creates it: people of action."

Plying yet further into our phone conversation to make his point about the importance of taking action, DiSalvo touches upon the deep meaning of Friedrich Nietzsche's essay on the use and disadvantage of history from his *Untimely Meditations*. In this lesser-known volume, the German philosopher invokes a clever incantation borrowed from Johann Wolfgang von Goethe to castigate those who would learn the hard lessons of history and yet fail to take personal action in pursuit of positively impacting culture: "I hate everything that merely instructs me without augmenting or directly invigorating my activity," Nietzsche quotes.

He continues:

> These words are from Goethe, and they may stand…at the beginning of our meditation on the value of history. For its intention is to show why instruction without invigoration, why knowledge not attended by action, why history as a costly superfluity and luxury, must, to use Goethe's word, be seriously hated by us—hated because we still lack even the things we need and the superfluous is the enemy of the necessary.

Embodying Nietzsche's concept of invigoration, David DiSalvo sits quietly, like a ticking time bomb, in his corner coffee shop possessing the same bold spirit as the German philosopher, living the truth of every word in his books and articles—even as he writes them. Not unlike thousands of his readers perched precariously alongside the intoxicating abyss of self-doubt, DiSalvo is similarly plagued by a chorus of neurally transmitted feedback loops, biochemically produced at the door to his own wall of indecision. In this sense, he is a cultural warrior fighting on behalf of his readers, practicing what he preaches.

In this regard, DiSalvo is the quintessential "pragmatic adapter," although certainly not the world's first, and he makes good use of current findings in scientific research to validate his claims well before he makes them. But he is also a bleeding-heart poet with a gift for prose that pulls the reader to the brink of decision in a J. D. Salinger, *Catcher in the Rye* sort of way without ever preaching the absolute gospel of anything. For example, a neologism like "pragmatic adaptation" is not solely an abstract concept from the author's commodious vocabulary. DiSalvo accompanies the term with the cracked mirror of his own self-reflexive will to overcome cerebral obstructions in his own tumultuous life. He only coined the term because *he is that term*—or more accurately stated: he is *becoming* that term.

Another one of DiSalvo's favorite sayings is *focus forward*, and every time he uses it in casual conversation I can recollect his admonition to me fifteen years ago (during a crisis of my own making) to *resolve into strategy*. Taking his advice then, I am reminded, now, exactly how important it was to hear him say these words in order for me to find the will to actually *do* it. As a consequence, memory of DiSalvo's admonition from years past provides the academic in me with a profound sense of confidence when I consider the science that underscores the simplicity of his sometimes seemingly prosaic and commonplace delivery.

"You've effectively used your metacognitive awareness to change the situation," he penned in *Brain Changer*, Chapter 2, and he's right. But this time around—fifteen years from the time he first inspired me to take metacognitive action—*resolve into strategy*—DiSalvo's admonition to focus forward into self-imposed patterns of *knowing*, *doing*, and *expanding* is supported with real scientific data. And all this suggests that he, too, is at least tangentially responsible for the positive results related to my "changed brain." Therefore, I cannot escape the logical denouement that an author is also party to a reader's redemption, however one chooses to define it.

"When we speak of 'mind,'" he writes, "we are speaking of an interrelationship between our brain, our mind, and the relationships we have with others' minds."

To quote Dr. Daniel Siegel,

> The mind [is] an emergent property of the body and relationships [and] is created within internal neurophysiological processes and relational experiences. In other words, the mind is a process that emerges from the distributed nervous system extending throughout the entire body, and also from the communications patterns that occur within relationships.

In the end, one must conclude that David DiSalvo is either hiding artfully behind the rhetorical veil of "science-help," his new term hinged on a novel synthesis of contemporary approaches to Theory of Mind—and even I am a sucker for his Dionysian intentions (perhaps the greatest sucker)—or that his suggestion that "I is not *me*" but, really, "I is *we*" is truly borne out in the scientific data, and that it demands that I end my own personal cult of narcissistic intentionality and actually connect with other human beings in the collective culture-building process of shared intentions. This would explain why DiSalvo confessed to me in a recent phone chat that he needs his readers as much as he hopes they need him.

Surprisingly, DiSalvo's observation that core elements of evolutionary development in the human brain have neither been naturally selected for multitasking nor for social isolation suggests that choosing to spend large chunks of time focused on the interests of others might actually be good for me—without violating the natural order of things. This is a fantastic takeaway from any book.

Finally, it is this courageous attitude on the part of its author—this Spartan will to take informed action, come what may—that makes *Brain Changer* a fitting corollary to *What Makes Your Brain Happy*. All that remains is a bit more room on my bookshelf for a third volume in a DiSalvo trilogy that defines what a "changed brain" looks like in the social context, and what one can ever expect to achieve in a developing global context of cultural disintegrations at so many local levels.

Perhaps DiSalvo can be persuaded to battle the gods of biochemically induced self-sabotage one more time in service to his readers, and tell us what it might feel like in a world beyond culture to be the last brain standing.

—Donald Wilson Bush, *Los Angeles, CA*

ACKNOWLEDGMENTS

WRITING A BOOK like *Brain Changer* is an intensely collabora-
tive effort that wouldn't be possible without the dedication of
researchers around the world working through the complex
subjects of human thought and behavior. The number of researchers
at universities, private laboratories, and public agencies I relied upon
for information to populate these pages is too numerous to list, but as
you read through the book and notes you'll no doubt notice citations
for one after another. I consider this book a brick-lined tunnel leading to new understandings about how our minds function, and every
brick represents a contribution from a researcher working tirelessly
to address crucial questions that expand our awareness.

I would like to especially acknowledge Jena Pincott, who gener-
ously agreed to write the foreword. Her work is among the very best
in science journalism, and it is a sincere honor having her words open
the book. Special thanks are also more than deserved by my friend
and collaborator of more than 20 years, Donald Wilson Bush, who
both illustrated the book and wrote its afterword. His range of skills
and breadth of knowledge qualify him as a true polymath—able to
both visually grasp and translate complex technical topics, and also
verbally elucidate challenging material like few people I've encoun-
tered in my life.

Others who helped along the way include my friend John Shade
Vick, whose grounded perspective aided in keeping me tethered to

the tangibles, and Bob Vandervoort, who was a steady friend and supporter every step of the way.

Major thanks also go out to my agent, Jill Marsal, a steadfast supporter and ally, without whom I would not be doing what I do. Thanks also to the editorial staffs at *Forbes* and *Psychology Today*, with whom I've had the pleasure of working for the last few years and hope to continue for many more.

I would also like to acknowledge everyone at BenBella Books who published this title. Working with the BenBella team is a joy, and I am exceedingly happy to be collaborating with such an experienced, insightful, and pleasant group of professionals.

Enormous love goes to my kids, Devin, Collin, and Kayla—the three best reasons I have for achieving anything in this life. I love you three more than I could ever capture with words.

A final word of thanks goes to my dad, Louis DiSalvo, to whom this book is dedicated, and who left the world far too early. He taught me how to think critically and showed me that the easy answers are frequently not the right ones, no matter how enticing they may seem. His friends called him "Lucky Lou" because he was a notoriously formidable poker player—but the truth is that his smarts outpaced his luck by a mile. He was a good man, and a tremendous thinker. This one's for you, Dad.

EXCERPT FROM DAVID DISALVO'S
THE BRAIN IN YOUR KITCHEN

THE BRAIN IN YOUR KITCHEN

WHAT CAFFEINE REALLY DOES TO YOUR BRAIN

I recently stopped drinking coffee. Yeah, I know, why would anybody do that? For me it was a combination of health-related reasons, and overall I can say I'm happy I did. If you had asked me a few days after I kicked it, though, I would have told you it was one of the dumbest things I ever even thought of doing—that is, if my head stopped pounding long enough to answer you in a complete sentence.

This radical life adjustment made me curious about caffeine and its effects on the brain, so I did some research. The most surprising thing I found was that caffeine doesn't really jack up the volume in our brain the way most of us think it does—the story about how our favorite drug works isn't nearly so straightforward.

First, what caffeine does not do.

Caffeine does not, by itself, make you a super productive, super fast, super talky jitter machine. That venti Café Americano is not the sole reason you're able to cram six hours of work into forty-five minutes, or that you're shockingly charming between the hours of 8 to 11 A.M.

What caffeine does do is one heck of an impersonation. In your brain, caffeine is the quintessential mimic of a neurochemical called adenosine. Adenosine is produced by neurons throughout the day as they fire, and as more of it is produced, the more your nervous system ratchets down.

Your nervous system monitors adenosine levels through receptors, particularly the A1 receptor that is found in your brain and throughout your body. As the chemical passes through the receptors, your adenosine tab increases until your nervous system pays it off by putting you to sleep.

The remarkable talent of caffeine is to mimic adenosine's shape and size, and enter the receptors without activating them. The receptors are then effectively blocked by caffeine (in clinical terms, caffeine is an antagonist of the A1 adenosine receptor).

This is important not only because by blocking the receptors caffeine disrupts the nervous system's monitoring of the adenosine tab, but also because of the players who make an appearance as this is happening. The neurotransmitters dopamine and glutamate, the brain's own home-grown stimulants, are freer to do their stimulating work with the adenosine tab on hold, and that's the effect you feel not long after downing your triple shot skinny mochachino.

In other words, it's not the caffeine that's doing the stimulating. Instead, it's keeping the doors blocked while the real party animals of the brain do what they love to do.

As every good coffee drinker knows, this effect lessens over time. It steadily takes more and more caffeine to achieve the same level of stimulation from your excitatory neurotransmitters. This is the irritating dynamic we all know as "tolerance."

The reason it seems that coffee and tea became a morning ritual is that caffeine helps fight off the sleepy feelings we're left with after a night of paying off a full adenosine tab. That's something our favorite legal drug is quite proficient at doing.

What it's not so good at doing, though we'd like it to be, is keeping us chugging away no matter how much sleep we miss. For a little while it might seem like caffeine is warding off sleep deprivation, but the effect won't last. Eventually the nervous system wins.

Of course, these effects vary depending on many things, including body type, weight and age. For some one cup of coffee will help kick things up; for others it might take three cups. And as mentioned, tolerance of caffeine is a major variable no matter what source you prefer for your drug of choice.

So if you decide to kick the habit, how long will it take to work through withdrawal? That depends on how much caffeine you routinely consume, but for the average two- or three-cup-a-day coffee drinker, expect up to ten days of symptoms like headaches, fatigue and a general feeling of wanting to shout loudly into peoples' faces.

Originally published on Forbes.com, July 26, 2012

ABOUT THE AUTHOR

DAVID DISALVO is a science writer and public education specialist working at the intersection of science, technology, and culture. His work appears in *Forbes, Psychology Today, Scientific American Mind, The Wall Street Journal, Mental Floss, Salon, Slate, Esquire,* and other publications, and he is the writer behind the widely read science and technology blogs, *Neuropsyched, Neuronarrative,* and *The Daily Brain.*

His first nonfiction book, *What Makes Your Brain Happy and Why You Should Do the Opposite,* has been translated into seven languages and is available worldwide. He is also author of the e-book *The Brain in Your Kitchen.*

Please visit www.brainchangeronline.com for more information.

NOTES

Preface

1. The story told in the Preface is true, although the names have been changed. I observed the story firsthand from beginning to end, as it involved close friends who were generous enough to allow me to use the details of the story in print.

PART I: KNOW

Introduction: Brain Changing—The Mind Shift Has Begun

1. Marc Lewis, *Memoirs of an Addicted Brain* (New York: PublicAffairs, 2012), 66.
2. David DiSalvo, *What Makes Your Brain Happy and Why You Should Do the Opposite* (Amherst: Prometheus Books, 2011), 17.

Chapter 1: Metacognition—The Impassive Watcher in the Tower

1. Robert J. Marzano, *Dimensions of Thinking: a Framework for Curriculum and Instruction* (Washington, DC: National Education Association, 1988), 278.
2. Ibid.
3. I am indebted to Thomas Goetz's article, "Harnessing the Power of Feedback Loops," which appeared in *Wired* (June 2011), for an outstanding explanation of how feedback loops operate across a range of disciplines, and for the best phraseology to describe the elements of a feedback loop (Evidence, Relevance, Consequence, Action) that I came across in my research. The article was accessed online: http://www.wired.com/magazine/2011/06/ff_feedbackloop/.

4. Stephen M. Fleming and Raymond J. Dolan, "The Neural Basis of Metacognitive Ability," *Philosophical Transactions of the Royal Society B: Biological Sciences* 367 (2012): 1338–1349.

5. Ibid.

6. Robert Kurzban, *Why Everyone Else Is a Hypocrite: Evolution and the Modular Mind* (Princeton: Princeton University Press, 2011), 35–37.

7. In his book, *A User's Guide to the Brain* (New York: Pantheon Books, 2001), physician John J. Ratey describes the "four theaters of the brain," which sets the stage for my use of the term "mental theater." Although the contexts in which Ratey and I use similar terminology are quite different, Ratey deserves credit for crafting a useful metaphor of mind. 341.

8. In his book *The Happiness Hypothesis* (New York: Basic Books, 2006), Jonathan Haidt provides examples of "moral dilemmas" that cause reasonable people to pause without having a well-defined reason for why they are offended. In particular, he presents the case of a brother and sister who decide to have protected sex—an example that most people react to with disgust, but since there is no outward repercussion for anyone except the two people involved in the act, it's not easy to explain why the example stirs so much moral outrage. Haidt's point is that we "feel" the outrage without relying on a reasoned explanation of why it exists.

9. Leonard Mlodinow, *Subliminal: How Your Unconscious Mind Rules Your Behavior* (New York: Pantheon, 2012), 17.

10. Timothy Wilson, *Strangers to Ourselves: Discovering the Adaptive Unconscious* (Cambridge: The Belknap Press of Harvard University Press, 2002), 24–27.

11. Ibid.

12. Fleming and Dolan (2012).

13. James M. Haynie, "Cognitive Adaptability: The Role of Metacognition and Feedback in Entrepreneurial Decision Policies" (doctoral thesis, University of Colorado at Boulder, 2005), 237–265.

Chapter 2: Mentalization—The Original Mind Game

1. Michael Gazzaniga, *Human: The Science Behind What Makes Us Unique* (New York: Ecco, 2008), 49.

2. Pierce J. Howard, *The Owner's Manual for the Brain,* Third Edition (Austin: Bard Press, 2006), 47.

3. Daniel J. Siegel, *The Developing Mind: How Relationships and the Brain Interact to Shape Who We Are,* Second Edition (New York: Guilford, 2012), 3.

4. Leonard Mlodinow, *Subliminal: How Your Unconscious Mind Rules Your Behavior* (New York: Pantheon, 2012), 87–88.

5. Ibid.

6. In their book *Self-Esteem* (Oakland: New Harbinger Publications, 2000), authors Matthew McKay and Patrick Fanning describe in great detail

various forms of the inner voice and how it shapes our behavior. For a more trenchant analysis on this point, I recommend consulting *Self-Esteem*.

7. Janet Metcalfe and Lisa K. Son, "Anoetic, Noetic and Autonoetic Metacognition," in *Foundations of Metacognition*, ed. Michael J. Beran, Johannes L. Brandl, Josef Perner, and Joëlle Proust (New York: Oxford University Press, 2012), 289–301.

8. In Chapter 9 of his book *Finding Flow: The Psychology of Engagement with Everyday Life* (New York: Basic Books, 1997), author Mihaly Csikszentmihalyi introduces the "Autotelic Personality," which he describes as a person who engages in an activity for its own sake, with the experience of the activity as the main goal. While this concept is significantly different from what I am calling the "Autonoetic Personality," it's certainly worth consulting *Finding Flow* for added dimensions of a personality working at the highest levels of self-awareness and invested in achievement of goals not only to attain them, but also to gain as much from the experience of attainment as possible.

Chapter 3: Pragmatic Adaptation—Changing Thinking, Changing Life

1. For an investigation into the evolution of seemingly basic human emotional responses, I recommend the work of neuroscientist Antonio Damasio, in particular his book *Self Comes to Mind: Constructing the Conscious Brain* (New York: Vintage, 2012).

2. A comprehensive discussion of "cultural evolution" can be found in the Stanford Encyclopedia of Philosophy: http://plato.stanford.edu/entries/evolution-cultural/.

3. Information on RNA nanotechnology comes from multiple interviews I held with research faculty at the University of San Diego School of Medicine for a confidential white paper during 2012.

4. Norman Doidge, *The Brain That Changes Itself: Stories of Personal Triumph from the Frontiers of Brain Science* (New York: Penguin Books, 2007), 150.

5. Moheb Costandi, "Researchers Watch Brain Rewire Itself After Stroke," *Neurophilosophy* (blog), July 2, 2008, http://neurophilosophy.wordpress.com/2008/07/02/researchers_watch_brain_rewire/.

6. Christopher J. Boyce, Alex M. Wood, and Nattavudh Powdthavee, "Is Personality Fixed? Personality Changes as Much as 'Variable' Economic Factors and More Strongly Predicts Changes in Life Satisfaction," pre-publication paper accepted for publication in *Social Indicators Research* (2011), 3.

7. Ibid.

8. Ibid.

9. Daniel Nettle, *Personality: What Makes You the Way You Are* (New York: Oxford University Press, 2007), 9, 10, 29.

10. Ibid.

11. Boyce, Wood, and Powdthavee, (2011): 33.

12. Walter Bradford Cannon, *The Wisdom of the Body* (New York: W. W. Norton & Company, 1932), 9.
13. Refer to definition of "allostasis" in *Part III: Expand Definitions.*
14. For an extensive discussion of thinking errors, please consult David Burns's book, *Feeling Good: The New Mood Therapy* (New York: Harper, reprint edition, 2008), 32–43.
15. Jeffrey M. Schwartz, MD and Rebecca Gladding, MD, *You Are Not Your Brain: The 4-Step Solution for Changing Bad Habits, Ending Unhealthy Thinking, and Taking Control of Your Life* (New York: Avery Trade, 2012), 201–202.
16. Gillian Butler and Tony Hope, *Managing Your Mind: The Mental Fitness Guide* (New York: Oxford University Press, 2007), 68–70.

Chapter 4: Tracing the Narrative Thread—The Power of Scripting and Salience

1. Daniel Dennett, "The Self as a Center of Narrative Gravity," in *Self and Consciousness: Multiple Perspectives*, ed. Frank S. Kessel, Pamela M. Cole, Dale L. Johnson, and Milton D. Hakel (New York: Psychology Press, 1992), 103–15.
2. The terminology "natural" and "adaptive styles" is frequently used in personality assessment tools, particularly in the DISC Index.
3. An excellent definition of "salience" in psychological parlance is found in the Blackwell Reference Online: DOI: 10.1111/b.9780631202899.1996.x.
4. For an excellent discussion of self-narrative and the therapeutic potency of narrative, I recommend Timothy Wilson's book *Redirect: The Surprising New Science of Psychological Change* (New York: Little Brown, 2011).

Chapter 5: The Mindscape—Looping it All Together

1. Albert Camus's famous quote about intellectuals was made in *Notebooks (1935–42)*, published in 1962, and republished by Marlowe & Co in 1998.

PART II: DO

1. Ron and Marty-Hale Evans, *Mindhacker: 60 Tips, Tricks, and Games to Take Your Mind to the Next Level* (New York: Wiley, 2011), 340–350.
2. Charles Duhigg, *The Power of Habit: Why We Do What We Do in Life and Business* (New York: Random House, 2012), 60–63.
3. Pierre J. Magistretti, Luc Pellerin, and Jean-Luc Martin, "Brain Energy Metabolism: An Integrated Cellular Perspective," *Psychopharmacology: The Fourth Generation of Progress* (Brentwood: American College of Neuropsychopharmacology, 1995), 657–670.
4. Shlomo Breznitz and Collins Hemingway, *Maximum Brainpower: Challenging the Brain for Health and Wisdom* (New York: Ballantine Books, 2012), 157–166.
5. As reported in *Live Science*: http://www.livescience.com/5406-chewing-gum-touted-diet-strategy.html.

6. A. Scholey, C. Haskell, B. Robertson, D. Kennedy, A. Milne, and M. Wetherell "Chewing gum alleviates negative mood and reduces cortisol during acute laboratory psychological stress," *Physiological Behavior* 97 (2009): 304–312.

7. K. Kamiya, M. Fumoto, H. Kikuchi, T. Sekiyama, Y. Mohri-Lkuzawa, M. Umino, and H. Arita, "Prolonged gum chewing evokes activation of the ventral part of prefrontal cortex and suppression of nociceptive responses: involvement of the serotonergic system," *Journal of Medical and Dental Sciences* 57 (2010): 35–43.

8. Chris Berdik, *Mind Over Mind: The Surprising Power of Expectations* (Current Hardcover, 2012), 66–68.

9. Ibid.

10. Research by psychologists David Watson and Lee Anna Clark is described in *Your Creative Brain: Seven Steps to Maximize Imagination, Productivity, and Innovation in Your Life*, by Shelley Carson (Harvard Health Publications / Jossey-Bass, 2010), 208–210.

11. Carson, *Your Creative Brain*, 209.

12. Dan Ariely, *The (Honest) Truth About Dishonesty* (New York: HarperCollins, 2012), 245.

13. Daniel J. Siegel, *The Developing Mind: How Relationships and the Brain Interact to Shape Who We Are*, Second Edition (New York: Guilford, 2012), 40–45.

14. Andrew Newberg and Mark Robert Waldman, *Words Can Change Your Brain: 12 Conversation Strategies to Build Trust, Resolve Conflict, and Increase Intimacy* (New York: Hudson Street Press, 2012), 128–136.

15. For a detailed explanation of brain wave biofeedback, I recommend consulting *A Symphony in the Brain: The Evolution of the New Brain Wave Biofeedback*, Revised and Expanded Edition. (New York: Grove Press, 2008) by Jim Robbins.

16. Matthew A. Sanders et al., "The Gargle Effect: Rinsing the Mouth with Glucose Enhances Self-Control," *Psychological Science* 23 (2012): 1470–72.

17. Carson, *Your Creative Brain*, 171–173.

18. Daniel Amen, *Change Your Brain, Change Your Life* (New York: Three Rivers Press, 1998), 150–171.

19. The tips on getting a better night's sleep are extracted from an article I wrote for *Forbes Magazine Online*: http://www.forbes.com/sites/daviddisalvo/2012/10/11/10-reasons-why-you-cant-sleep-and-how-to-fix-them/.

20. Gillian Butler and Tony Hope, *Managing Your Mind: The Mental Fitness Guide* (New York: Oxford University Press, 2007), 129–133.

21. Mark Hyman, *The UltraMind Solution: The Simple Way to Defeat Depression, Overcome Anxiety, and Sharpen Your Mind* (New York: Scribner, 2010), 265–266.

22. Information in this section is extracted in part from an article I wrote for *Forbes Magazine Online*: http://www.forbes.com/sites/daviddisalvo/2012/08/07/the-10-reasons-why-we-fail/.

23. As reported by the University of Connecticut Health Center: http://today.uconn.edu/blog/2013/04/alcohol-research-center-battles-addiction-with-science/.

24. Information for this section was extracted in part from an article I wrote for *Forbes Magazine Online*: http://www.forbes.com/sites/daviddisalvo/2012/08/28/10-reasons-why-some-people-love-what-they-do/.

25. The example given in Number 22 was adapted from my previous book, *What Makes Your Brain Happy and Why You Should Do the Opposite* (New York: Prometheus Books, 2011), 158–160. Paul Thibodeau and Lera Boroditsky, "Metaphors We Think With: The Role of Metaphor in Reasoning" *PLoS.ONE* 6 (2010), online access journal.

26. Daniel Pink, *A Whole New Brain: Why Right-Brainers Will Rule the Future* (New York: Riverhead Books, 2005), 139, 152.

27. Koenraad Cuypers et al., "Patterns of receptive and creative cultural activities and their association with perceived health, anxiety, depression and satisfaction with life among adults: the HUNT study, Norway," *Journal of Epidemiology and Community Health* 133 (May 2011): 66–71.

28. Helen J. Huang, Rodger Kram, and Alaa Ahmed, "Reduction of Metabolic Cost during Motor Learning of Arm Reaching Dynamics," *The Journal of Neuroscience* 32 (2012): 2182–90.

29. Information for this section was extracted in part from an article I wrote for *Forbes Magazine Online*: http://www.forbes.com/sites/daviddisalvo/2012/06/21/the-five-hallmarks-of-respected-achievers/.

30. As reported by the University of Colorado Boulder's Department of Integrative Psychology: http://www.colorado.edu/news/releases/2012/02/09/perform-less-effort-practice-beyond-perfection-says-new-cu-study.

31. Information extracted from an article I wrote for *Psychology Today Online*: http://www.psychologytoday.com/blog/neuronarrative/201009/why-running-is-incredible-medicine-your-brain.

32. Daniel J. Siegel, *Mindsight: The New Science of Personal Transformation* (New York: Bantam Books, 2010), 9–13, 38.

33. V. S. Ramachandran, *The Tell-Tale Brain: A Neuroscientist's Quest for What Makes Us Human* (New York: W. W. Norton & Company, 2012), 250–255.

34. Howard Gardner, *Five Minds for the Future* (Boston: Harvard Business Review Press, 2009), 1–10.

35. Edward de Bono, *Six Thinking Hats* (New York: Back Bay Books, 1999), 1–26.

36. Aaron T. Beck, Arthur Freeman, and Denise D. Davis, *Cognitive Therapy of Personality Disorders* (New York: The Guilford Press, 2004), 30.

37. Nicholas Humphrey, *Soul Dust: The Magic of Consciousness* (Princeton: Princeton University Press, 2012), 49.

Appendices

1. A version of this essay originally appeared on *Psychology Today Online*, February 7, 2012: http://www.psychologytoday.com/blog/neuronarrative/201202/what-is-science-help.
2. A version of this essay originally appeared on Forbes *Magazine Online*, August 21, 2011: http://www.forbes.com/sites/daviddisalvo/2011/08/21/why-we-need-pragmatic-science-and-why-the-alternatives-are-dead-ends/.
3. A version of this essay originally appeared on Forbes *Magazine Online*, August 8, 2011: http://www.forbes.com/sites/daviddisalvo/2011/08/08/why-scientists-and-journalists-dont-always-play-well-together/.

INDEX